# SPARKS
# FROM THE APOSTLES

Saint Paul

AUGOUSTINOS N. KANTIOTES
*Bishop of Florina, Greece*

# SPARKS
# FROM THE APOSTLES

## ORTHODOX HOMILIES ON THE
## SUNDAY APOSTOLIC READINGS

*And take . . . the sword of the Spirit,*
*which is the word of God.*

—Ephesians 2:17

*Translation and Foreword by*
ASTERIOS GEROSTERGIOS

INSTITUTE FOR BYZANTINE AND MODERN GREEK STUDIES
115 GILBERT ROAD
BELMONT, MASSACHUSETTS 02178

*Sparks from the Apostles* appeared in Greek under the title Ἀπόστολος, published by the Orthodox Missionary Brotherhood, " Ὁ Σταυρός"("The Cross"), Athens, 1973. The author dedicated this book to "the listeners and readers of these Sermons." We dedicate this translation to all the clergy, the Sunday School teachers and to all the faithful of the English-speaking Orthodox Church in the Diaspora.

All rights reserved.
Copyright © 1992, by Asterios Gerostergios
Published by the Institute for Byzantine and
Modern Greek Studies, Inc.
115 Gilbert Road, Belmont, Massachusetts 02178, U.S.A.

Library of Congress Catalog Card #: 91-76723

*Printed in the United States of America*

Clothbound ISBN 0-914744-92-5

# CONTENTS

# TRANSLATOR'S FOREWORD

Through the grace of God, we were able to bring into the light of day this book of sermons on the Sunday Epistle readings by the venerable Augoustinos N. Kantiotes, Bishop of Florina, Greece. The bishop's previous book of sermons, *Drops from the Living Water*, is already slaking the spiritual thirst of many hearts. Glory be to God!

Bishop Augoustinos, a distinguished preacher and acclaimed writer, addresses both the anxieties and the needs of our time through his homilies. In an Orthodox manner, he discusses the spiritual, ethical, and social problems that beset contemporary man. With his homilies, which are based on the Bible and on the preaching of the Apostles, he tries to strengthen the people of God in their Christian attitudes and conduct. His message is convincing, and he delivers it in a lively, well written, yet simple and comprehensible way, using both historical and contemporary examples. He brings the Epistle readings to life, and in his own unrivaled fashion, he transports the reader back to those first heroic days of the Apostles.

The bishop speaks with pious enthusiasm from a heart full of faith and fervor. He warms the hearts of his readers by bringing to life that first heroic Christian era. He strikes sensitive chords of the heart, creating a spiritual atmosphere in which the Word of God embeds itself firmly. At the same time, he demonstrates that the message of the Bible is a great and unique gift from heaven to earth, from God to man.

Just like the recently published book, *Drops from the Living Water*, the present volume, *Sparks from the Apostles*, constitutes an act of love, not only to our Orthodox people but to all who are interested in the pure Orthodox teaching of the Bible. Most especially, it is offered to students and preachers of the Holy Word, to clergy and laity alike, to strengthen them in their homiletic and catechetical roles in the Church. May God bless this spiritual seed sown in the field of the Lord, the English-speaking Orthodox Church all over the world.

The translation and publication of this book were difficult and costly. In fact, publishing it would have been impossible without the moral and financial support of co-workers and spiritual children. They were many. We especially thank our beloved Father Steven Yankopoulos for assisting us. To all who helped, we express our warm appreciation. May our Lord reward them out of the bounty of His divine gifts.

Asterios Gerostergios

# PREFACE

Last year we published a book entitled *Sunday*. In it, we collected all of our short homilies on the Gospel excerpts read on Sundays during the year. They were written in a simple language.

That book, a small compilation of Sunday sermons, was meant to serve the people of our diocese. Our priests, poorly educated as they are, have it as a handy reference. Our villagers, either when they hear the priest read from it during church services or when they read it themselves at home, understand it and are pleased. It is easy spiritual food to digest. Because of this, the book *Sunday* was well received, not only in our diocese but outside of it, too. Priests from other dioceses order *Sunday* and use it. Even lay people read it and are spiritually uplifted by it. We're informed that even abroad, where Orthodox Greek Christians live, the book is in circulation. An educated and pious clergyman, who serves a community in America, translated it into English to help his parishioners.

The reception of the book *Sunday* by both the clergy and laity encouraged us to continue our humble effort and to write a second volume of homilies based on the Apostolic excerpts read on Sundays during the year. These sermons were first printed in the form of pamphlets and were read every Sunday by the priests and then given to those attending church services free of charge. Because the clergy and laity asked for these homilies, we are publishing this new series in this present book entitled *Sparks from the Apostles*. As we wrote in the preface to the book *Sunday*, these homilies are a few drops from the immortal water of the Lord's teaching. They will bring some refreshment to simple souls who thirst for the word of God.

We rejoice in this new offering and glorify God, Who enables us to communicate again with the greater portion of our much suffering people in a plain and unaffected language. As for those few educated people who wish for more sophisticated language, we admonish them to read Corinthians 1:19-2,8. There are, however, educated people and even scholars, who hear the simple word of God and are pleased, because they love our people who do not have advanced education, and they appreciate simple preaching that everyone can understand. The word is like bread—bread for all. So preaching must be, also.

Florina March 25, 1973
The holy day of the Annunciation.
+ Augoustinos, Bishop of Florina

# SUNDAY BEFORE EPIPHANY
2 Timothy 4:5–8

## MY CHILDREN, KEEP YOUR FAITH

*I have fought the good fight, I have finished the
course, I have kept the faith.*
—2 Tim. 4:7

Today, beloved, the Apostle speaks. Which Apostle? As
you all know, Christ's disciples, the Apostles, numbered
twelve. One of those twelve, Judas, betrayed Him. But
besides these twelve disciples and Apostles of Christ,
there was another Apostle, whom Christ did not call as
He did the others when He was here on earth. Not until
Christ was already in heaven did He call this other
Apostle. And who was the Apostle who received the call
from heaven? It was Paul.

Before Christ's call, Paul considered Christ his
enemy. He hated Christ, just as he hated all Christians.
Whenever he heard that there were Christians in the
area, he would capture them and bring them before the
archpriests and scribes to be judged, just as Christ had
been judged and condemned. Paul didn't limit his search
for Christians to Jerusalem; he traveled to other cities in
pursuit of them. He became a terrible persecutor of
Christians.

But all of a sudden—and who would expect it? Who
would imagine it?—Paul, the one who on hearing
Christ's name would foam with hatred, came to love no
other name on earth more than he loved the name of
Christ! Upon uttering Christ's name, his heart would
beat with ardent love, and his eyes would fill with tears.
"Christ, I thank you," he would say, "for I was a sinner,
the greatest sinner, and You came and saved me."

Why did Paul change? How did Paul's enemy become his friend? How did this persecutor of Christians become a disciple and Apostle of Christ? A miracle took place. And whoever wants to learn about this miracle should open up the New Testament and read the Acts of the Apostles, chapter 9.

From the time that Paul believed in Christ, was baptized in His name, and became a disciple and Apostle of Christ according to the command he received from Him, he started to travel the world and to preach about Christ. And where didn't he go? Where didn't he preach? Like an eagle with golden wings, Paul flew to the east and then to the west. His apostolic mission lasted twenty-five years.

Finally, Paul went to Rome. There, the idol worshipers, the enemies of Christ, arrested him and threw him into prison. From day to day he waited for the iron door of the jail to open—not so that he would be freed, as had happened on so many other occasions when he had been imprisoned—but so he would be taken out and executed. Nero, the evil king of Rome who hated Christians with a passion, every day took thousands of Christians from the prison and killed them. Some he had beheaded; others he had thrown to the lions or into the fires; still others he ordered covered with pitch and set on fire to become torches for lighting the streets, squares, and palaces of his kingdom. Those days were terrible, but they were also days of glory for Christ's faith.

Paul was in prison, knowing what awaited him. Someone else in his place would have been very depressed. But Paul, though he waited for death from hour to hour, was full of joy! Death did not frighten him. Paul believed that the life of a man does not end in the grave; only the body ends in the grave. Paul knew man is more than matter. Man is also a spirit, an immortal soul, which, once it is liberated from the body, goes to another world where souls reside. And is this place pleasant or unpleasant? The answer depends on the way the person lived here on earth. Believers will go with believers, and unbelievers, with unbelievers. Alas to the one who in the few years of his or her life lives without believing and with corruption. And joy to the one who lives with faith and good works.

If there was anyone who lived with faith in Christ and carried out good works, it was Paul. With his preaching, he opened the eyes of thousands of people who lived in sin, disbelief, and corruption. Paul's dedication to God and the love he had for his neighbor were of a degree that the world had never before seen. Through his example, Paul proved that the teaching of Christ can be applied, that Christ gives power to His weak creatures to become heroes, and that Christ lives and reigns in the hearts of His faithful followers. Through the miracles that he performed in the name of Christ, Paul proved that the religion that he preached is the only true religion in the world.

As Paul waited for martyrdom in prison, he must have looked back on the years that had passed, on his life from the time that he had believed in Christ. Cities and villages, home to the men, women, and children who believed in Christ because of his preaching, must have passed before the eyes of his soul. Paul would have seen that the fight that he fought to spread the Gospel to the nations did not fail, but instead brought results. Where once there was not even one Christian, there were now many. And what Christians! They were loyal Christians who were ready to shed their blood for Christ. In the lands of idolatry, which were full of thorns, poisonous snakes, evils, and passions, churches were growing. They were actual gardens of Christ, spreading their fragrances everywhere.

Paul, feeling full of gratitude toward Christ, Who had helped him in this sacred task, wrote a letter from prison—the last letter he ever wrote. He wrote to a disciple whom he loved very much. This disciple, who had followed Paul everywhere, helping him in his apostolic work, and was now far away in Asia Minor serving as the Bishop of Ephesus, was Timothy.

"My child," Paul wrote to Timothy, "in a little while I will leave this world. I will suffer martyrdom. I will shed my blood for Christ. I have fought the good fight, I finished the race, I kept the faith. Now I await the crown of glory—the crown that the Lord will give not only to me, but to all those who love Him and wait for Him to come again."

This voice, beloved, this voice of Paul passes through the centuries and reaches us. And we—who through the preaching of the Apostle Paul believe in Christ—we, too, are Christ's spiritual children. Just as our fathers and forefathers believed in and fought for Christ's glory, in the same way we must also fight for the glory of Christ. Paul's voice comes alive again and can be heard by the ears of all: "Children of Greece, children of Macedonia, which I loved so much, fight the good fight, preserve the faith. Many enemies are trying to snatch it away. Close your ears to these voices. Hold tight, all of you, to the Orthodox faith. In this faith the fathers found consolation and light. In this they relied during the harsh days. Remain in this faith. Outside of this faith there is only the lie and deceit. For this faith, fight to the death."

## ABOVE ALL THE HEAVENS

*He that descended is the same also that ascended up far
above all heavens, that he might fill all things.*
—Eph. 4:10

In our times, beloved, people have a great mania for travel. They're not satisfied to stay in one place. They always want be on the move, to see new countries, to enjoy natural landscapes, and to meet other people. Look at what's happening with tourism. Thousands of airplanes fly thousands of tourists around and around the world. And lately, it seems, there are some who have had their fill of trips on earth and want to travel beyond it, to the moon and other planets, on what are called interplanetary journeys. Already the first travelers have reached the moon, and now they are trying to reach Mars and the other planets.

If we could but stop and think that there aren't 100, 1,000, or 2,000 stars but millions and billions of stars; if we could but realize that these stars are a very great distance from the earth and that if we were to make a spaceship that travels like lightning, at the speed of light, we would need not thousands but millions of light years to reach the most distant stars; if we could but comprehend these things, our minds would be dazzled and we couldn't help but admire the unreachable grandeur of

Divine Creation. We would kneel before the Creator, and we would say the words that David said—those same words that famous astronomers who study God's majestic skies now repeat: "The heavens declare the glory of God, and the firmament proclaimeth the work of His hand." (Psalm 18, 1)

Truly, how foolish are unbelievers and atheists! They are like the young man who didn't believe in God and said that everything we see is created by chance. The young man's friend made a large globe like the globes that are in schoolrooms and placed it in his unbelieving friend's room when he wasn't there. When the unbeliever returned to his room and saw the globe, he immediately asked his friend: "Who brought this here? Who made it?"

"No one made it!" his friend answered. "It came by chance to your room."

"What are you saying?" replied the atheist with astonishment. "Only someone who's crazy can say that the globe came here by chance."

"Oh, my friend," the atheist's friend answered, "if he who says that this globe, which is a worthless, small toy, was created by chance is crazy, then how much crazier is someone who says that the millions of stars, the enormous globes or planets, were created by chance, without thought, without the wisdom and the strength of God?"

Unbelief cannot stand when a person thinks logically. Reason says that someone built a house, that a machine that is in motion was started by someone, and that this endless house, which we call the heavenly world, with its countless stars, was made by someone, and that someone put this huge machine into motion. He is the all-wise, all-good and all-powerful God.

But why are we talking about stars and space travel? We are talking about them because the Apostle Paul gives us the opportunity. And why, you are wondering, the Apostle Paul? You are thinking that at the time of the Apostles there were no airplanes, no rockets, no spaceships; people traveled by donkey, and no one imagined they could reach the moon and the stars.

Yes, this is true. But we have to know that besides the earth, besides the moons and the stars, besides the heavens that we see, there is another heaven—a heaven that no one can see with a telescope, a heaven that no one can reach with rockets and spaceships. It is not physical but spiritual. It is not imaginary but real. And just as you are sure there is a moon, stars, and a sun, be assured that this spiritual heaven exists. In this heaven is God. In this heaven is the Holy Trinity: the Father, the Son, and the Holy Spirit. And in this heaven are the angels and the archangels, the immaterial spirits, and the souls of the saints.

Today's Epistle speaks of this heaven, the spiritual one. It describes someone to whom we might refer today as the king of the astronauts. He is, of course, the Lord Jesus Christ. And to you who are amazed at the space travels of the astronauts: Come and see the journey that Christ took. From the heavens He came to earth. For thirty years He lived on our planet. For three years He performed miracles. He was crucified and descended into Hades. He fought with death and won. He came out of the dark kingdom of Hades victorious and triumphant. And afterwards—oh Christ, who can describe Your grandeur!—He was lifted up from the earth. He arose on high to ascend beyond the sun and the stars. He went beyond all of the heavens to where divinity dwells.

And what then? Did Christ stop caring about people? Even beyond the heavens, He is very close to us, closer than anyone else. He is next to us and enlightens us. He warms us, comforts us, supports us. He gives us the strength to be victorious. He gives us all of the means for our spiritual formation. We will find these means for our salvation plentiful, if we wish, in the kingdom He established here on earth: the Church. Oh the Church! In the Church, heaven with all its stars lowers, and the earth becomes heaven. Again man is elevated and reaches heaven, where Christ is, above all heavens. To Him belongs glory, honor, and adoration.

Are there those of you who hear us speak like this and think we speak about fantastic and unreal things? If so, it is because you don't believe, because you haven't tasted Christ and the Christian life. To believe in Christ, take into your hands the Holy Writ and read its message, read the Epistles of Paul, start to go to church, and listen with piety to the Divine Liturgy. Then you will feel that, although your soul at first flew low and always saw and was amazed at worthless things, now your soul flies very high with new wings; it sees all that at first it could not see and hear; it hears all that it did not listen to before; and it bows down and venerates the Creator Who created the natural and supernatural world—those things that we see and those things that we do not see—and says: "How magnified are Thy works, O Lord! In wisdom hast Thou made them all; the earth is filled with Thy creation." (Psalm 103, 26)

## IT NEEDS UPROOTING

*But now ye also put off all these: anger, wrath, malice,*
*blasphemy, filthy communication out of your mouth.*
—Col. 3:8

The Apostle Paul, beloved, writes to the Colossians, who were residents of a large city in Asia Minor. Before they believed in Christ, the Colossians were idolaters. Prostitution, adultery, and every kind of evil fouled their city and all the other cities of idol worshipers. For centuries, these sinful practices had characterized the heathen ethos. This evil was like a huge tree that had sent its roots into the hearts of a corrupt people and could not be uprooted.

Whoever dared to challenge the false gods of the Colossians and to attack their sinful customs was considered an enemy to be judged and condemned to death. Socrates was an example of someone who was condemned to die because he dared to speak about religion. Socrates didn't reform the idolaters; nor did the other pre-Christian philosophers. Instead of diminishing, the evil among the Colossians worsened as time passed.

However, what the ancient philosophers didn't accomplish in those parts of Asia Minor, the word of God did. Yes, the word of God, preached by the Apostle Paul and his disciples. Together, they accomplished a miracle: The Colossians stopped worshiping idols.

Idolatry, however, is like a tree that leaves some roots in the earth when it falls; if they are not pulled out, they can send up new shoots. Idolatry does the same thing. Like a tree that no one expected to fall, idolatry had sent its roots into the ancient world. Paul cut the tree with the power of the word, and idolatry fell. However, some of the vices and evils of the idolaters sent up new shoots. Customs that were not Christian but instead were reminiscent of idolatry appeared here and there. Some people, even though they were baptized in the name of Christ and promised publicly to renounce the devil and all human passions and evils, started again to pollute themselves with prostitution, adultery, moral corruption, obscenity, and blasphemy. This regression brought great sorrow to the Apostle Paul, who yearned for the Christians to progress on the road to Christian living. Paul thus admonished them in his epistle to step away from evil.

Just as one throws away an old and unclean garment and puts on a new one, in the same way one must cast off the old and unclean garment of the corrupt life of the idolater and put on the new garment of Christ: the new life, the Christian life, the virtues that Christ had. The way Christ lived is how every Christian should live. This is why, when people are baptized, the Church sings: "As many of you as have been baptized into Christ, have put on Christ." It is as if the Church is saying, "Don't dirty your new clothes, the clothes of Christ, with awful sins. Keep your body clean from prostitution and adultery, your tongues clean from filthy language and blasphemy, and your hearts clean from wrath, anger, and greed. Drive every evil and sin far away." Listen again to the words of the Apostle Paul in today's Epistle: "But now ye also put off all these: anger, wrath, malice, blasphemy, filthy language out of your mouth."

All of the evils that Paul mentions unfortunately exist today, but with one difference. In Paul's time, transgressions were few. Yet even those few transgressions drew an immediate reaction from other Christians who did not tolerate the existence of prostitutes, adulterers, thieves, and foul-mouthed, blasphemous people. But today? Alas! Evil has spread like an infectious disease, like an epidemic. The violations of God's commandments are everyday events. Even sadder, the reaction against those who violate God's law is nonexistent, or if it does exist, it is lukewarm. Where is the prophet? Where is the apostle? Where is the preacher? Where is the teacher of the Bible? Where are the Christians who will teach, counsel, contest, cauterize, and excommunicate?

Let us take as an example those who take the name of God in their mouth and blaspheme—not in secret or in the mountains and the valleys so as not to be heard by anyone, but in public, in the coffee shops, in the centers of amusement, on the streets, on buses, in the squares, everywhere. Many hear them. But no one is saddened or indignant; no one approaches the blasphemer to offer counsel and to say a few words such as, "What are you doing? God gave you a tongue to glorify Him and to thank Him for all the blessings He gives you every day, every hour, every moment! Yes, every moment your heart beats is a blessing from God. You should thank Him for the infinite love He shows you. You should glorify Him for His majesty, for all that beauty that you see and enjoy on earth. But instead of thanking Him, you open your mouth and blaspheme His name, something even the devil doesn't dare blaspheme. By blaspheming, you become worse than Satan. Do you think that you'll remain unpunished?" Listen to an example. A farmer, who used oxen to plow in the field, blasphemed God. Immediately, one of the oxen bellowed terribly, escaped from the plow, and turned against the blasphemer with its horns. The blasphemer barely escaped death. Others came running and saved him. From then on the farmer stopped blaspheming. An ox had taught him that he must respect God Who made everything.

Beloved! Step on Satan and defeat him. Uproot every evil from your heart, especially blaspheming, which the Ten Commandments mention. Keep your mouth clean of blasphemy. Protest when you hear others blaspheming. Let everyone hear: Whoever blasphemes God shall be punished sooner or later.

## WHAT ARE YOU READING?

*Give attendance to reading.*
—1 Tim. 4:13

The Apostle Paul, beloved, had many disciples. They were persons who believed in Christ and were baptized. Their hearts burned with their fervent love for Christ. They followed Paul throughout his apostolic journeys and helped him in his work. Being so close to the great Apostle, these disciples became small apostles. The Church owes a great deal to those disciples of Paul, who, after Paul's martyrdom, continued to preach of Christ in different places.

One of Paul's disciples, who never left him and always remained true to the apostolic mission, was Timothy. Paul ordained Timothy Bishop of Ephesus, one of the largest cities of Asia Minor. It was in Ephesus that Timothy suffered a martyr's death because he was opposed to some carnivals that took place in that city. Are you listening, you who want to have carnivals, to dance, to sing shameful songs, to get drunk and roll around on the ground like animals on the holy days of Lent? If you don't want to listen to your bishop, listen to St. Timothy, who protested not only with his words but with his blood.

St. Paul wrote to Timothy to give him certain advice, even though Timothy was no longer one of his disciples. As a bishop, Timothy had a responsible seat in the Church and was obligated to direct the spiritual progress of all Christians. He had a duty to support the weak, to comfort the sorrowful, to instruct the young and old alike, and to censure those who misbehaved. He had a duty to protect Christ's flock from the wolves who were ready to attack and take the sheep. The sheep are the Christians, and the wolves are the heretics, the people who reject the teachings of the Bible.

Oh, how delicate and how difficult is the position of a bishop! What responsibilities a bishop has for his flock! What will he say to God if even one soul is lost because of him! And because the writer of this book is a bishop—a bishop in a difficult age of unbelief and corruption—I beg you to pray for me. Those of you who love Christ and want His work to progress in our district, I beg you with tears in my eyes not to forget me in your prayers. Pray and say, "Christ, help Bishop Augoustinos." If Paul needed the prayers of his Christians, how much more do we!

One of the pieces of advice that Apostle Paul gave to Timothy, was this: "Until I come, attend to [your] reading, to exhortation, to teaching." "My son," says the Apostle Paul, "I recommend that you read Holy Writ. When you read it, all of your attention must be on what you are reading. You must be careful and diligent. And from this book you must take examples to console those who sorrow and to teach those who are shaky in their faith and have need of spiritual support."

The advice, beloved, "Attend to reading," was not just written for Timothy, the Bishop of Ephesus, but for all bishops, all clerics, and all people, men and women.

Yes, Paul is addressing every Christian today when he wrote: "Attend to reading." Paul said it to Timothy. But if he lived today, Paul would have said it not once but thousands of times for today's Christians, both clerics and laity. He would shout at them: "Watch what you read."

In Paul's time, books were scarce and very expensive. Today, millions of books circulate everywhere. Most are inexpensive and can be found in everyone's homes. Books and magazines clutter not only the mansions of the rich but also the homes of the poor. Everyone reads. Unfortunately, however, many of the books that circulate among the people are not beneficial but harmful—that is to say, they are scandalous and can corrupt the soul. Those who read these books are in great danger of being scandalized, losing their faith, having their character corrupted, or being terribly injured. Yes, a book written by a faithless and corrupt author can destroy a soul. These evil books are written with such skill that they draw people, just as the bait of the fisherman lures the fish. These books are the bait of Satan. They are the destroyers of people, especially the young, who are not in a position to judge which books are of value and which are harmful.

Unfortunately, people are not careful enough about what they read. When they are getting ready to eat, they are careful. If they sense the food has spoiled and they are in danger of being poisoned, they don't eat. How can people be careful about what they eat but careless about what they read? Without realizing it, people who read books of atheism and unbelief are swallowing the poison that is in them—a poison that is sugar-coated.

Beloved! A wise man once said that if someone could go to hell and see those who were condemned, he would hear many of them crying, groaning, and saying that the start of their destruction was the reading of a book: "This book destroyed me. Cursed is the hour I took it in my hands to read!" And on the other side, if someone could go to paradise and see there those people who rejoice and enjoy the beauty of paradise, he would see and hear countless souls who would say that the beginning of their salvation was the reading of one book, the Bible: "Let that hour be blessed, and thrice blessed, that this book fell into my hands to read and to do what it advised me to do."

Brother! Listen to the Apostle Paul: "Attend to your reading." Throw those indecent books and magazines from your hands. I beg you, throw them into the fire before they burn you. Pick up the Holy Bible and read it day and night. This is the book, the only book, that can save you if you believe in it.

# THE ROCK OF AGES

*Jesus Christ is the same yesterday, and today,and for ever.*
—Heb. 13:8

Yesterday, today, tomorrow. Into these three words, beloved, time is divided. And how quickly time passes! Today becomes yesterday, and tomorrows today. Time is like a river that flows night and day. It runs all the time. Time is like water. If you were to wade into the river, you would realize that the water that touches your body only touches you for a moment and immediately leaves; more water touches you and moves on, and so on and so on. If you were to stay in the water for an hour, the water would change a thousand times, even though the river seems the same. This is what happens with time. Like a continuously running river, one moment succeeds another moment; an hour, an hour; a week, a week; a month, a month; a year, a year. And so the years pass: the infant becomes a child; the child, a teenager; the teenager, an adult; the adult, a white-haired elder. Although everything changes, time continues on its course. Until when? Only God knows.

Yesterday, today, tomorrow! Yesterday represents the years that have passed. It is 1991 that just departed. Yesterday it was 1990, 1989, and so on. And going backwards continuously, we recall various dates, some of which left vivid memories in our hearts, pleasant or unpleasant. Thus we arrive at World War II—at the historic date of October 28, 1940, the day our small country said no and fought in Northern Epirus for liberty. And going back further, we reach 1914 and World War I. Then to 1912, when the Orthodox people of the Balkans united to defeat the Ottomans and liberate their lands from slavery. If we continue going back, we can review other events, such as the Greek Rebellion in 1821, the appearance of Napoleon, the French Revolution, the independence of America, the fall of Constantinople, and many other historic occasions.

We can go back all the way to 1 A.D.—to the year when out of the depth of the darkness of the ancient world the star of Bethlehem arose: Christ, the savior of the world, was born. And if we want to continue our journey to the years prior to Christ, we will recall still other events and persons. We will see that for three hundred and more years one flag flew over all of the world—the flag of the Roman Empire. Before the Roman flag, another flag flew—the flag of the empire that Alexander the Great, the Macedonian, established. Before Alexander the Great, we see the kingdoms of the Persians, the Babylonians, and the Egyptians.

And going still further back, we meet the most ancient people of the world: Adam and Eve. Does time stop there? No. Before Adam and Eve, there were other events, such as the creation of the planets, the sun, the moon, and billions of stars. All this took place within time. When exactly, we don't know. Science cannot determine the exact date. What we do know is that all of this constitutes yesterday. History concerns itself with yesterday.

But there isn't only yesterday. There is also today. People learn about what is happening today from newspapers, radio, and television. With what thirst people follow the things that are happening today! Yesterday—the things that have passed—does not interest them. But they have to be sure  that those who will live a hundred to two hundred years from now will not be interested in what they are doing today.

Few are those who are not absorbed with today but instead open up history books and read about what people did in years past. Most people have their minds on the present. What shall we eat, what shall we drink? What shall we see today at the movies and on television? All for today. They have forgotten yesterday. These people have even forgotten their mothers and fathers, who died just yesterday. They never visit their graves to say a prayer or leave a few flowers. The dead, they say, are dead, and the living are alive. These people are concerned about today—not about where they come from or where they are going. Too many people live for today—not as spiritual people but as materialists whose motto is, "Let's eat and drink, for tomorrow we die."

Yesterday, today, tomorrow! And there are others who leave the past and present, the yesterday and today, and turn with anxiety toward tomorrow. What's going to happen? Will we have peace or war? Are we going to be well or incurably sick? Will we live happily or unhappily? What's going to become of our children? These people are always uneasy. The future occupies them, and they are prey to fortune tellers, astrologers, and mediums who find the right moment to predict the future for them.

But why are we saying all of this? Why are we speaking about things that have passed? Why do we speak about today and about tomorrow? Because today's Epistle, for the holy day of the Three Hierarchs, tells us about someone who existed yesterday, who exists today, who will exist tomorrow, and who will exist forever. Of the billions who lived yesterday, that is to say in the past, some were glorified, but all eventually died and were forgotten. Those of us who are living today will tomorrow not be living; a grave waits for us. Still others are not yet born. They will be born tomorrow, that is to say, in the future, and they will live a certain number of years in order to die and become yesterday.

Oh my Christians! In this unbreakable stream of time, which passes and carries away people like the leaves that fall from the trees in autumn—in the middle of that channel of time, One remains. He remains like the rock, which although assaulted on all sides by waves, remains unshaken for ages and ages. Time, which our ancient ancestors called all-subduing because it defeats and destroys everything, cannot do anything to Him. Yesterday, today, and tomorrow He is the same. Of course, He is Jesus Christ.

People! Fall down and worship Him! He is our God. In Christ our fathers believed. In Christ the Three Hierarchs, those great fathers of the Church, believed. Of Christ they preached with all of their strength. They brought the knowledge of God to the world. And today, which is their holiday, they cry to us: "Believe in Christ!"

We also believe in Christ today. In Christ the new generations will believe tomorrow. Christ is the rock of ages. Those who believe in Christ with all their heart are like the man who built his house on a rock. Let all the rivers fall upon him. Let all the waves strike him. Let all the demons wage war against him. Those who believe in Christ are secure. Christ "is the same yesterday and today and forever."

# SUNDAY OF THE PRODIGAL
1 Corinthians 6:12–20

## A BEAUTIFUL TEMPLE

*What! Know ye not that your body is the temple of the Holy Ghost which is in you, which ye have of God, and ye are not your own?*

—1 Cor. 6:19

Religion, my beloved, isn't a creation of the priests for the purposes of exploitation, as unbelievers and atheists would say. No. Religion is the noblest of feelings. It is something that is planted inside the hearts of people. And whatever is planted inside the heart, no one can uproot. The feeling of religion is natural, like the feeling a mother has for her child. No one could order a mother to abandon her feelings for her child. A mother will love her child, and even under threat of death, her last words will be: "My child, I love you." Religion is the same. Religion is a feeling deeply rooted in man. Who can uproot it?

From the day man appeared, religion appeared. Wherever archaeologists dig, they find signs of religion. They find ruined temples and marble plates that speak about religious rites and sacrifices. They find statues and idols that the ancients worshiped. Historians and philosophers will confirm that wherever you go, you will find that religion is the first necessity of man. You can find a city that doesn't have schools, hospitals, and other buildings, but you won't find a city that doesn't have a temple or people who practice religion. Religion is everywhere. Altars and sanctuaries are everywhere. Temples are everywhere. When the Hebrews, one of the most ancient people of the world, found themselves in the desert going toward their homeland, they built a movable temple like today's mobile home, and the priests prayed and offered sacrifices to God in this mobile temple. Afterwards, when they arrived at Palestine and settled there, King Solomon built the famous Temple of Solomon. This temple became a pilgrimage site for Hebrews from all over the world. They came to celebrate the great feast of Passover. Today, all that remains of this temple are some ruins. At those ruins, which remind one of the ancient glory, Hebrew men and women come every Saturday to pray and cry because of the temple's destruction and to ask God to help them rebuild it. Thus the true prophesy of Christ about this temple came true—that it would be destroyed and not a stone would remain on a stone. (Luke 21:6)

The Hebrews were not the only ancient people to build temples. The Egyptians, the Persians, and the Babylonians also built grand temples. But the most important temple built in antiquity by the idol worshipers was built by our ancient forefathers, the Greeks, on the Acropolis. It is the Parthenon.

Later, the Christians came. But the Christians couldn't build temples during their early years because the Christians were being persecuted. The kings and emperors who didn't believe in Christ not only didn't allow the Christians to build churches but also didn't even want to hear the name of Christ. To worship God the Christians had to leave the city at night and go to caves. And even there they weren't safe. If they were discovered, their persecutors collected brush, blocked the entrances of the caves with it, set fire to it, and burned the Christians. Not until Constantine the Great became the first Christian Emperor were the Christians allowed to build churches. St. Helen, Constantine's mother, built a magnificent church in Jerusalem, where Christ was crucified. Later, the Emperor Justinian built the Church of the Holy Wisdom. Today, there are churches in all Christian lands. In large cities and in the smallest villages, among the huts of the villagers and herdsmen, church bells ring calling Christians to prayer.

Thousands of beautiful churches are built in the various lands of Christendom. If you ask which is the most beautiful church of Christianity, some would answer the Church of the Holy Wisdom in Constantinople; others, the Church of St. Peter in Rome; still others, the Church of St. Paul in London. But you, my beloved Christians, what do you say? What is the most beautiful church in the world?

Opening today's Epistle reading and hearing those inspired words, we learn that besides those churches which we've mentioned—churches built with stones and mud—there is another church that has a much greater value than all the other churches we have mentioned. This church, as today's Epistle reading tells us, is the body of the person who believes in Christ. Those who don't believe also have bodies, but because of their filthy practices with prostitution and adultery, their bodies have become like dirty stables. Before they believe and repent, people are dirty and stinking stables. But those who repent and weep because of their sins are the ones who are baptized in the waters of the holy baptismal font or in the tears of repentance and confession. They wash themselves and are cleansed of their sins and become as white as snow. And their bodies become temples where the Holy Spirit resides.

So a person becomes the temple of the Holy Spirit! What a blessing, what an honor, what an attainment. Unfortunately, today's Christians don't appreciate the significance of this honor that Christ gave them. They continue to sin and fall into the frightful sins of adultery and prostitution, dirtying their flesh. They are careful not to dirty their clothes, but not so their bodies. They become especially filthy during the beginning of Lent when they get drunk and don't know what they're doing.

My Christians! If someone were to tell you to go to church and do some awful thing, you would not do it. And if you saw someone else doing awful things in church and making it filthy, you would not tolerate it because you want the church to be clean. Thus, in the same way that you want the church in your village to be clean, you must want your body to be clean—clean of fornication, clean of adultery, clean of every unclean practice.

A body clean of sins is a church. The Holy Spirit comes into that church and lives there. The soul prays and worships God in that church. It worships Him every day, every hour, and every minute. When Sunday comes and the bell rings, then the Christian runs from one church to the other, to public prayer—the prayer that takes place in the churches of the villages and cities.

## MEAT-FARE SUNDAY
1 Corinthians 8:8–9:2

## NO SCANDALS

*Wherefore, if meat make my brother to offend, I will eat no flesh while the world standeth, lest I make my brother to offend.*

—1 Cor. 8:13

Man, my beloved, is free—free to do whatever he wishes. Yes! But along with freedom God gave man reason, a conscience, and law to judge those things that he is going to do. Man should not live without judgment, without thought, without conscience, and without God's law. And because of this, man ought to ask himself every time he is about to do something, "Should I do this? Is it reasonable? Is it good and beneficial to all? Does reason allow it Does my conscience approve of it?" And above all, "Does the law of God, the Gospel, which is above everything else, permit it?" If the answer is yes, then go ahead and do it. If, however, the answer is no, then don't do what evil desires, passions, bad and corrupt friends, and Satan are urging you to do. Don't listen to them. They don't want what's good for you; they want your destruction.

Man! Submit yourself and your freedom to the will of God; you will not lose your freedom. No, you will save it, and it will grow, and you will become a truly free man. Those who say that they are free because they submit to all the desires of the flesh and all the sinful desires of the world are not free but slaves who are pulled wherever those evil desires wish to go, just as the circus trainer pulls the bear by the ring in its nose.

Some things, such as murder, fornication, adultery, stealing, and all that God's law condemns, are sinful, and we should stay away from them. Other things don't seem sinful, so people don't avoid them but do them without their conscience bothering them.

Today's Epistle mentions one such example. In ancient Corinth, many believed in idols and worshiped false gods. To appease these false gods, they offered herds of cattle, oxen, and sheep. They slaughtered the animals and offered them as sacrifices. From the slaughtered animals the priests would take a piece of meat and put it on the altar; they would light a fire and burn the meat. The smoke would rise upward, and the smell of the meat was enough, the priests said, to satisfy the gods. The rest of the meat the priests would distribute to the people like a blessing from the gods. These meats were called sacrificial meats, or "meats offered to the idols."

Unfortunately, the gods for whom the ancient Corinths sacrificed whole herds of sheep and oxen were false, and the sacrificial meats had no blessing. They were no different from the other meats that were sold at the butcher shops. Because of this, most Christians, who believed in the true God, considered them like any other meats and didn't think anything of eating them. Some Christians, however, thought that they shouldn't touch these sacrificial meats; if they saw some Christian eating them, they would be scandalized. A dispute arose among the Christians. Some feared that weak Christians would be carried away by idolatry and begin to eat the sacrificial meat, thinking of it as special meat that had the blessing of the false gods upon it. Other Christians ate the sacrificial meat without a guilty conscience. Who, then, was right and judged correctly? The second judged correctly and did right, because, as we said, the gods were false, and what blessing can a false god give? None.

Yes, the Apostle says to them, your judgment is right, and you are free to eat the sacrificed meat; but as long as some of your brother Christians do not have the same opinion as you, you shouldn't eat the offerings. After all, love is above all else—the love that makes us think not only about ourselves but also about others. Thus, there are situations in our lives when we should sacrifice our rights in order not to hurt or scandalize others. "Never," cries Apostle Paul, "will I eat meat-offerings if I will scandalize my brother."

How sensitive was the Apostle Paul's conscience. He avoided not only the sins that the law of God condemned but also those things that weren't sinful but might scandalize weak Christians who were not in a position to think on as high a level as he. Paul was afraid of scandals. What can we say now about today's Christians who don't take anything into account and don't think about what kind of impression a particular action is going to make on their neighbor, or who break God's commandments and before the eyes of people do things that scandalize the community?

Scandal-makers are many. Here's one: It is Wednesday and Friday. It is Lent. It is Holy Week. It is Good Friday. Does the Christian fast? No! He ignores those days of fasting, eating meats and other prohibited foods in front of others and claiming that fasting is no longer important. Here is another one: It is Sunday morning, and people are going to church. But he is sitting at a coffee-house, smoking and talking with others. Here is a third: He stops at the bar, gets drunk, and goes home at midnight and abuses his wife and children, waking up the neighborhood. Here's a fourth: He threw his lawfully married wife out, abandoning her, and now lives unlawfully with another woman. Here's a fifth one: He opens his obscene mouth and blasphemes Christ, the cross, the Virgin, and all of the saints. The examples are endless.

All those who openly break God's commandments are guilty not only of the sin they commit but also of the scandal they create by their bad examples. The consequences of their actions become even greater when these people are well known in the community and in a position to influence other people.

You who are parents, you who are teachers and professors, you who are community leaders and government officials, you who are scholars and scientists, and most of all, you who are priests of the Most High, watch your behavior very closely. Be careful not to let down the people who follow your good example. A bad example is a scandal. A bad example is like someone throwing rocks onto a highway and endangering passing cars that can run into the rocks and veer out of control, causing injury and death to the occupants. How accountable are those who threw the rocks? Very accountable. And even more accountable are those who, by setting a bad example, scandalize those they influence.

## CHEESE-FARE SUNDAY
Romans 13:11–14; 14:1–4

# NIGHT-DAY

*The night is far spent, the day is at hand: let us therefore cast off the works of darkness, and let us put on the armor of light.*

—Rom. 13:12

The Apostle today, my beloved, is crying: "My brothers and sisters! Why are you sleeping? The night is far spent. The day is near at hand. Awake. Get dressed and get ready for the new day." This is what the Apostle cries out today. Whoever hears him would think that Paul is speaking about natural things that all of us know. For who doesn't know what night is and what day is? "Night is coming," "day is coming" are words that all of us say every day. Day ends, night comes. This is the way time passes between night and day. Only those people who were born blind live constantly in darkness, in an endless night, and don't know what day means. Oh, but how the blind would want to open their eyes if only for one day and see all the beautiful things we see. Unfortunately, we don't appreciate our gift of sight as we should.

The Apostle Paul, however, does not speak of day and night with the meaning we are familiar with. Just as our Lord Jesus Christ used images and examples from the natural world and the everyday lives of people to teach, the Apostle Paul speaks and teaches in the same way. He teaches with images and examples. But what can Paul have meant by saying night and day? This we shall see in today's homily.

Paul refers to the life that we live here on earth— from the moment we're born until the moment we die—as night. Night? Yes, night. Indeed, there are certain similarities between night and our earthly life. What are they? Just as darkness dominates in night, and only the stars and the moon light the earth a little bit, in the same way darkness dominates this present life. It is not a natural darkness, as is the darkness of night, but a moral and religious one. Sin, error, and impiety are darkness. To examine what people think, say, and do would be to see that the world lives in sin. Like a thick fog, sin hides the sun, and people don't see the truth. Falsehood dominates. Immorality, fornication, adultery, and every other uncleanliness triumph in human societies. Theft, robbery, greed, avarice, and a wild exploitation of people by people in spite of all the laws and the courts spread the black shadow to cover all the world. There isn't one person who doesn't groan at the injustice. Darkness is greed and avarice. Darkness is a hatred that dominates. Darkness is a vengeance that pushes nations to war. There is little love. What love there is, is like a small light that threatens to go out in the storm of the dark night; the cold grows, hearts freeze, and people live as though they were at the North Pole, which is in darkness most of the year. Oh sun! Why do you delay in appearing? Come and warm our bodies and souls again!

The present life is called night because of the sin that spreads throughout. But it is called night for another reason, too. At night, it is difficult to distinguish people —are they known or unknown? Friends or enemies? For example, we have heard of a man shooting and killing his own brother in the middle of the night because he took him to be an enemy. When morning came and he saw he had killed his brother, he almost went crazy with sorrow. The same thing happens in this present life. Because of the hatred that prevails, people can't see the brother who comes from God—the common Father of all people—in the face of everyone. Day must come, and the sun must shine to dissolve the hatreds and passions for people to love each other again and for the peace of God to prevail.

There is one other similarity between night and the present life. At night, people dream in their sleep. Even though they are only dreaming, they think what's happening is real. Here's a dream: A beggarly and insignificant man wears rags and lives from alms. He falls asleep and dreams that he is a king dressed in gold, that he wears a crown on his head, that he lives in a palace, and that everyone bows down before him. The beggar is a king! But he can't enjoy it for very long. He wakens, and then he realizes that it was only a dream and nothing more. Something like this happens in the life we live. There is, for example, a king. He lives many years in a palace, even a half century. He receives honors, glory, and riches. But now comes death. Then the eyes of the soul open, and he sees all that he enjoyed in the world was a dream.

Yes, life is a dream! And because of this, during the funeral service, when the casket is in the church, our Church calls us to think and philosophize on the vanity of human life. It chants: "Where is the pleasure of life which is unmixed with sorrow? Where is the glory which on earth has stood firm and unchanged? All things are weaker than a shadow, all more illusive than dreams; comes one fell stroke, and death in turn prevails over all these vanities. Wherefore in the light, Oh Christ, of Your countenance, and in the sweetness of Your beauty, to him whom You have chosen grant repose, for You are the Friend of Mankind."

Our present life is night, then. And what is day? It is that other, future life—the life that starts at the moment of death and continues without interruption to eternity. What is this present life before that life? A shadow, a dream. And yet so many labors, so much effort for this shadow and this dream. We labor and toil as though we expect to stay here forever. And we are indifferent to that other life which is coming today or tomorrow to wake us from sleep and show us reality. Unfortunately, most people today don't believe there is life beyond death. For Christians, however, there shouldn't be any doubt. We have unshakable proof, which is worth more than all the proofs about the soul's immortality and future life that ancient and modern philosophers have given us. That great proof, of course, is Christ. Christ assures us that there is an eternal, future life. It is impossible for Christ to lie. Everyone else may lie, but only one doesn't lie: Christ. Beloved, as much as you are sure that tomorrow's morning will come, be more assured that this present life will be followed by eternal life. That is the bright day.

Oh life eternal: life near Christ, life near the angels and the saints, life full of gladness and spiritual joy, life brighter than the sun. Oh Lord, make us love this life and wish for it. And make us worthy, when we close our eyes in this earthly life, to receive us high in the heavens, in the eternal and blessed life, through the prayers of the Most Holy Theotokos (Mother of God) and all of the saints. Amen.

# THE FIRST SUNDAY OF GREAT LENT
## (SUNDAY OF ORTHODOXY)
### Hebrews 11:24–26, 32–40

## ARE YOU REVILED FOR CHRIST?

*Esteeming (Moses) the reproach of Christ greater riches
than the treasures of Egypt.*
—Heb. 11:26

Today is the first Sunday of Lent, the Sunday of Orthodoxy. An excerpt from the eleventh chapter of the Epistle
to the Hebrews is read in all churches. I ask you, beloved,
when Divine Liturgy is over and you go to your homes,
don't start talking about worldly things; instead, open up
your New Testament and read again the eleventh chapter
of the Epistle to the Hebrews. That chapter is a hymn of
praise. The Epistle opens the history of the Old Testament. It takes examples of men and women who believed
in the true God and, with this faith, succeeded in doing
things that no other human being could do. The faith of
these believers was so strong that it overcame every
obstacle and enemy and resulted in countless miracles.
    Which of these many miracles shall we talk about
here? Or which of these heroes shall we mention and
praise? If we have to narrate all the miracles of those
heroes, we would have to do not one but a hundred
sermons, and again they wouldn't be enough. Because of
this, of all the names that today's Epistle reading mentions, we will concentrate on only one name, the name
of Moses.
    Moses lived about 1500 years before Christ. His
life was full of miracles, the first one taking place during
the first days after his birth. According to one law that
the king of that time, the pharaoh of Egypt, had issued,
all newly born male children of the Hebrews were to be

killed and thrown into the Nile River. This satanic law was passed to exterminate the Hebrew race. Are you shuddering? And Satan, who induced a king to publish such a law, is today continuing his evil work. Alas! There is no longer only one pharaoh. Many claim to be pharaohs. They are countless. They are men and women who don't want to have children, and should a mistake occur and a child begin to grow in a mother's womb, they get rid of it through abortion. They are reprehensible people, even worse than the pharaohs. They throw other people's children into the river. They kill their own children. But God will punish them just as the pharaoh was punished. The pharaoh drowned innocent children, but he himself also drowned in the waters of the Red Sea with all of his army.

Moses, a Hebrew child, should himself have been killed when he was born, according to the pharaoh's law. But he wasn't killed. He was saved. How? His mother put him in a basket, which she covered with pitch so that the water wouldn't enter it. She gently placed the basket into the river, and it floated like a little boat. The pharaoh's daughter, who was walking by the river, saw the basket floating in the water, and she retrieved it. With astonishment she saw that inside the little basket was a baby boy. The princess liked the baby so much that she adopted him and raised him like a prince in the palace. He was an intelligent child, and eventually he became one of the most educated people of his time. He lived amidst riches and was destined to become the pharaoh of Egypt one day. What a fortunate child many of us would say!

One day, Moses left the palace and went to the desert. He became a shepherd and lived in the desert for forty years, until God called him for a great mission.

What a strange thing for a young prince to leave the palace and become a shepherd! Why? Because Moses knew even as a child that he was of Hebrew descent. He saw how much his nation suffered from the tyrants of Egypt. Moses was not an unfeeling man who looked only for the good life, ignoring the misfortunes of others. He was a noble person, and inside his soul there was a struggle. On the one side, the palaces, riches, choice foods, glories, honors, and all the worldly things tempted him. On the other side, the poor huts, the beatings, the imprisonments, and the hunger and misery of his slave compatriots saddened him. What should he do? Stay in the palace? To do so would make him a traitor, forsaking his faith and homeland for the good life. But to leave the palace and go with an enslaved people? How could one so used to the good life live the life of the humble and destitute?

Moses chose the second way. He chose poverty over riches, suffering over the easy life, dishonor and scorn over glory. Instead of being the beloved child of a princess, he became one of the children of an enslaved nation. Thus he left the palace, went to the mountain, and became a shepherd. Later, when God called him to become the leader of his race in the struggle for liberty, he proved faithful to his mission. There were times when the people showed Moses their worst behavior. When certain difficulties appeared in the struggle, the impatient and ungrateful people cursed and jeered Moses, their benefactor; for them Moses had sacrificed everything. And whatever the Hebrew people did to Christ when he came into the city to save it, they did the same thing to Moses. They insulted him as they also insulted Christ. But Moses endured it all. He knew in whom he believed and for whom he suffered all of this. He believed in God and remained true to his mission.

We, my beloved, should imitate Moses. It is better, my brothers and sisters, to be poor and despised for believing in Christ than to be rich and famous with the devil. It is preferable to be insulted and despised for believing in Christ than to be praised and honored  by the devil's children. Let us pay attention to this last point, because we live in an age of great unbelief and corruption. The world, if it sees someone believing in Christ, going to church, receiving the holy mysteries, and trying to live a pure Christian life, makes fun of that person, calling him or her out-of-date, old-fashioned, retrogressive, uneducated, foolish, stupid, crazy. Thus, many are afraid to admit they believe in God. Even small children are afraid to make the sign of the cross in front of adults who might ridicule them. Here is another example: a certain little one, at the end of a Divine Liturgy, approached me and very quietly whispered in my ear: "I want to become a priest!" And why, I asked him, don't you say it aloud?" "If I say it aloud," he said, "everyone will mock me." If you don't want them to mock you, my boy, don't become a priest. Instead, choose a profession that the world will honor and respect. So look at where we have come! In the future, the way we are going, only those who have the courage to be scorned for Christ will pledge their faith. They will be the imitators of Moses, who preferred to be insulted for his faith rather than abandon it and be honored in the royal palaces.

## THE SECOND SUNDAY OF LENT
## (FEAST OF ST. GREGORY PALAMAS)
Hebrews 1:10–14; 2:1–3

# ABOVE ALL CHRIST

*They shall perish; but Thou remainest . . . but Thou art the same, and Thy years shall not fail.*

—Heb. 1:11-12

We live, beloved, in a beautiful world. This beautiful world, which we see and enjoy, is a wonderful sight to behold. And what doesn't it have! It has plains and mountains. It has rivers, lakes, and seas. It has plants, flowers, and trees. It has fish, birds, and animals. Take birds, for example; what an amazing variety, from sparrows to eagles! The different kinds of birds are distinguished by their sounds, color, beaks, flight, nesting location, habits, length of life, and many other characteristics. It is the same with all animals, plants, flowers, and trees. They are each created with such perfection that the greatest scholars of the world marvel at them. Each species is like a factory that works with marvelous precision. For example, consider the nightingale, whose song we wait for each spring. If we were to weigh this songbird, we would find it weighed no more than an ounce. Yet this tiny creature is a small and lively machine—not a dead machine but an alive one that has all that is needed to move and work. It also has some fine chords in its larynx that enchant you when it sings. It is like listening to a guitar. What am I saying? Like an orchestra of various instruments. No musician can equal its music. And I ask you: is it possible that these things that we see here on earth are accidental? Who made matter? Who molded it so that it takes on different shapes? Who hid different attributes and strengths in this matter? Who enclosed such enormous power in a particle of matter that, if it were freed, could move thousands of railroad cars and ships? Who taught music to the nightingale? Who taught the bee to build its honeycombs with such skill, as though it were an engineer or an architect? Who taught the ant to make its underground dwellings and to work as an organized community? The questions are endless. There is, however one, and only one, logical answer: God!

Yes, the earth, along with all that exists and lives upon it, is God's creation. But is the earth God's only creation? No. The earth—this enormous planet that the astronomers tell us weighs billions of tons—this earth, if we compare it with the millions and billions of other heavenly bodies, is like a grain of sand, a drop in the sea. And again we ask: Who created these countless celestial bodies? Who gave them their first movement? Who set their courses so that they move inside the endless universe and do not hit each other? Who gave light to the sun? Who set the distance of the earth from the sun to be such that the earth is neither burned to a crisp nor totally frozen? Who set the course of all the stars? Again, the logical answer is God!

Everything is amazing! But something else is the most amazing thing of all. It is that God became a man and walked on this earth because of His infinite love for us. God's human incarnation is the miracle of miracles. Our Lord Jesus Christ is the God-man. He is God. He is the second person of the Holy Trinity. In cooperation with the Father and the Holy Spirit, He created the world. David proclaimed this great truth in the Old Testament, and the Apostle Paul repeats it in today's Epistle reading: "And Thou, Lord, in the beginning hast laid the foundation of the earth; and the heavens are the works of Thine hands." (Heb. 1: 10)

Our ancient forefathers marveled so much at creation that they considered all that they saw in this beautiful world to be divine. They made everything gods: the sun, the rivers, the seas, the plants, the animals, the birds. But this was a serious error. And the Word of God, Holy Writ, frees us from this error. It teaches us that the differences between God and His creations are enormous. God is immaterial, timeless, incorruptible. Matter, from which the universe is created, does not have these godlike qualities. Matter isn't eternal: it isn't incorruptible. At some point in time it started, and at some point in time it will end. The day will come when the sun, for example, which has lighted and warmed the world for thousands of years and seems eternal, will go out, just as a lamp goes out when there is no more oil. And the earth shall be destroyed, like all the planets, all the stars, and all of the material universe.

Although the physical universe will be destroyed, its creator, our Lord Jesus Christ, will continue to exist. No change will terminate His existence. That is why the Apostle repeats the words of David today and says: "They [the heavens] shall perish; but Thou remainest; and they all shall wax old as doth a garment. . . . But Thou art the same, and Thy years shall not fail."

A fundamental change shall take place in the material universe. A new world, which will be infinitely more beautiful than the one we see, shall come out of the destruction. And the creator of this new world shall again be our Lord Jesus Christ.

Christ is above matter, whatever form and shape it may take. He is above the sun and the planetary systems. Not only is Christ above the physical world; He is also far above all the spirits—much higher than people, even those who were distinguished for their wisdom and holiness. Who is, I ask you, the wisest, the holiest of people? No one when compared with Jesus Christ. Above all people of all centuries that have passed and the centuries that shall come—from Adam till the last person who shall be born and live on our planet—far above them is Christ. What am I saying? Christ is above the angels and archangels. And even these immaterial spirits recognize the indescribable grandeur of Christ; they fall and worship Him and sing the sublime hymn: "Holy, Holy, Holy Lord of Sabbaoth, heaven and earth are full of Your glory." This leaves only the demons and the unbelievers who don't recognize the authority of Christ. But even the day will come when even their power will be destroyed totally, and the power of Christ shall dominate everywhere.

O Christ! You are the true God. You are our Creator and Maker. You are the King of the universe. All creation bows before You. All angels and archangels worship You. And we humble and sinful creatures fall before You, venerate You, and ask for Your mercy. Yes, Lord, we ask for Your mercy.

# THE THIRD SUNDAY OF LENT
## (THE VENERATION OF THE HOLY CROSS)
Hebrews 4:14–16; 5:1–6

## ARE YOU PROCLAIMING (CONFESSING) YOUR FAITH?

*Brothers, let us hold fast our profession.*
—Heb. 4:14 King James

Today, beloved, on the third Sunday of Lent, the Epistle reading is an excerpt from a letter to the Hebrews, written by the Apostle Paul for Hebrews who believed in Christ. They were few compared to the rest of the Hebrews who, in spite of all the miracles that took place both before and after the Resurrection, refused to believe in Him. These unbelieving Hebrews became furious when they heard that some of their compatriots believed in Christ. They used every means, even the most criminal, to force them to return to Judaism. They beat them, jailed them, tormented them, took away their properties, and set fires to their homes. The Christian Hebrews who were persecuted by their countrymen were hungry, naked, and homeless. They needed consolation and support so as not to give up and deny their faith.

Now, who else was more suitable to console and support these Christians than the Apostle Paul? Paul, formerly a fanatic Hebrew who had persecuted his Christian countrymen with a passion, had changed fundamentally. Paul came to believe in Christ, was baptized, and became Christ's most ardent preacher. He who previously blasphemed Christ, now preached the word of God with courage and great power and professed Christ everywhere. He understood very well what these believing Hebrews were enduring. He understood their sufferings. He understood the ideological war that was being waged against them to shake their faith. With passages taken from Holy Scripture, which the enemies of Christ interpreted any way they pleased, with lies and with forgeries, the unbelievers attempted to prove that Christ was not the Messiah for Whom the Hebrew nation had awaited for centuries. For these reasons, Paul wrote his famous letter to his suffering Christian compatriots. Paul was being consoling and supportive. He proved that Christ is above the patriarchs, prophets, angels, and archangels. Christ is the Word of God, the Messiah, the redeemer of the entire world, the true God. Paul's arguments, taken from Holy Scripture, are indisputable. He rebuked unbelievers and told those who were not shaken in the faith by the attacks of the enemies to take courage and strength. Paul's Epistle to the Hebrews is a powerful weapon against all unbelievers of all times. At the same time it is a warm invitation to all Hebrews and all unbelievers to abandon their unbelief and believe in Christ.

In this Epistle, after proving that Christ is the true God, the Apostle Paul addresses everyone, saying: "Brothers, let us hold fast our profession," that is, let us hold fast to our faith in Christ, and let us preach it and confess it everywhere without reservation, without doubt, and without fear. We must be unshaken and brave as we profess our faith.

"Brothers, let us hold fast our profession." The faithful not only of that age but also of the following years when the Christian faith was persecuted, heard and practiced this counsel that was inspired by God. Whoever reads the martyrologies cannot help but stand in admiration before the heroes of the faith. They had only to say three words to the tyrants—"We deny Christ"—to be spared the torments, to be freed from the prisons, and to

be allowed to return to their homes. But they didn't say
these words. To the question of the torturers, "What are
you?" they answered, "We are Christians." The martyrs
professed their faith before thousands of people who
shouted, "Death to the Christians." It was very moving to
hear not only men but also women and even small
children say, "We believe in Christ. Do to us whatever
you wish. We won't deny our faith."

The history of our nation reveals that during the
Greek Revolution of 1821, when the Turks conquered the
island of Chios, they brought the women and children to
the seashore (the men had been killed in the fighting),
put a crucifix on the ground, and told them: "Whoever
steps on it will be saved; those who don't will be killed."
The Turks gave them some time to decide. But no one,
not a woman or child, stepped on the crucifix. They all
shouted: "We believe in Christ. Praise be to Christ, praise
be to the All-Holy Mother, praise be to the saints." In
this way, professing their faith, these new martyrs
sacrificed their lives.

"Brothers, let us hold fast to our profession." If from
those heroic times of Christianity we look at our present
day, will we meet the heroic spirit of the martyrs of our
faith? The kind of danger that existed when the unbelievers put knives to the necks of Christians, saying to
every one of them, "Either you deny your faith or you
will be killed," does not exist in our country today.
Unbelievers don't put the knife to the necks of the
faithful, but they wage war in another way: they scoff at
the faithful. And the so-called faithful are so timid that
they cower at the scoffings, as if the unbelievers were
ready to kill them. Alas! The martyrs weren't afraid of
the knives, the flames, or the other forms of torture.
Today, Christians are afraid of a mocking smile, a

scornful word, a frown; they tremble lest they be characterized as old-fashioned; they silence their voices and refrain from making the sign of the cross in public, hiding like little children playing hide-and-seek. They don't profess their faith.

Because the so-called faithful don't profess their faith, the unbelievers and impious, observing this lack of response from the Christian people and receiving no rebukes or chastisement for their scoffing, become bold and shameless, mocking the Orthodox faith and blaspheming the clergy. Wherever they may be, the unbelievers of today try to spread the lies of atheism. Where is Paul to profess the faith and rebuke the impious and faithless?

Where is Paul? You, beloved, must become Paul. We're not saying that you can measure up to Paul. No. But you can imitate Paul and the other Apostles and martyrs, and you can preach Christ within the small circle you live in. Don't be afraid. Even if all those around you are scornful, sarcastic, and jeer at your faith, even if they try with a thousand and one satanic means to shake you and pull you far from Christ, you must not lose your courage. Remain steadfast and unafraid like a rock that's unmovable, even though it is assaulted on all sides by the waves of the ocean. Your faith in Christ must be as solid as a rock, the Orthodox faith. With words, with deeds, and with your Christian life, you must profess in this unbelieving and atheistic world that your faith in Christ is the only true faith. Only then will you become like Paul, a martyr and confessor of Christ. Then you will be among those whom the Apostle today exhorts: "Brethren, let us hold fast our profession."

## THE FOURTH SUNDAY OF LENT
## (THE SUNDAY OF ST. JOHN CLIMACOS)
Hebrews 6:13–20

## WHERE DO YOU HOPE?

*Which hope we have as an anchor of the soul, both*
*sure and steadfast, and which entereth into that*
*within the veil.*

—Heb. 6:19

Those of you, beloved, who have traveled by ship know that ships, both large and small—and even the transoceanic ones that travel the seas and oceans—have an anchor. An anchor is a necessity. No ship starts on a voyage if it doesn't have an anchor that is in good condition. When storms arise and the ship is in danger of being swept onto the rocks by the waves, the captain orders the sailors to drop the anchor. Now, if the anchor catches on the bottom, then the ship won't be carried away by the waves. An anchor makes the ship safe in times of storm.

But why are we talking about voyages, ships, and anchors? Because today's Epistle reading speaks about an anchor. And what is this anchor that the Apostle says we ought to have? We will address this question in our sermon today.

The Apostle Paul speaks allegorically. He uses the anchor as an image, an example, to teach us. Let us talk about this image.

The life we live in this world, beloved, is like a journey. The start of our journey is the day we were born. The end of this earthly journey is the day we will die. The sea is the world. And just as the sea is not always calm but has days when strong winds and huge waves trouble it, in the same way the life we live in this world isn't always calm and serene. Few are the days in which we enjoy calmness and peace. Most of the time the waves don't allow us to have any peace and rest. The winds and waves are the sorrows and troubles of life. Which sorrows and which troubles? Can you count the waves of the sea? You can count many more troubles and sorrows of human life. Poverty, crime, sickness, desertions, infidelities, ingratitude, treacheries of friends, slanders and calumnies, injustices and persecutions, and plunderings and greediness are just some of the evils that can befall a person during his or her earthly life.

There are so many troubles and sorrows that times come when a person loses courage, is shaken, and resembles a ship that finds itself in a storm and in danger of foundering. Of course, the ship uses its anchor when struggling in heavy seas. But what does a person who is struggling against the sorrows and troubles of life need so as not to be destroyed? That person needs an anchor, too, and that anchor is hope. Without hope a person cannot live.

Now let us talk about the hope that keeps a person from sinking into the wild waves of despair. If we look at society, we will see that people base their hopes in different persons and things. Some people place their hopes in savings in banks, in real estates, or in their shops, factories, and ships. Some place their hopes in the protection of people who hold important positions. Others place their hopes in their bodily strength and good health, in their personal success, and in science. Still others place their hopes in their children, expecting their children to take care of them one day when they get old. And finally, there are those who place their hopes in political solutions, relying on great and powerful nations with whom they sympathize ideologically (like the Communists), to win and satisfy their aspirations. Is there any need for us to point out how deceptive and false these hopes are? Those of us who have passed through the years and had our hair turn white and are now walking toward the grave have seen so many changes in the past fifty years that we have gained a precious and instructive experience. We have seen greedy people who accumulated money and thought they didn't need anyone. They made money their god. They placed their hope in money. And then came the two world wars and overturned everything. The wars debased money, and one day the man who had a million dollars saw it lose so much value that he couldn't buy a loaf of bread. Bank certificates turned into worthless sheets of paper, good only for wrapping things. We saw houses destroyed by bombs, and villages and cities burned. We saw those whom people feared—generals, governors, and dictators of great nations—fall and become the weakest, dying dishonorably, suffering humiliating deaths, committing suicide, or being arrested and executed; their friends and admirers disappeared. We saw people who had been healthy and as strong as steel suddenly fall into bed and melt like a candle; they had once had the strength to crush stones with their hands and now couldn't lift up a spoon. We saw others, who had labored hard to raise children into responsible adults, become old and abandoned by their ungrateful offspring and left to find shelter in some home for the aged. We saw political parties dissolve and other new ones appear—and these become old and replaced by new ones: the wheel of the political machine runs continuously, and the up becomes down and the down, up.

What does all of this meant? It means that hopes based on people or things do not have a solid foundation. These hopes are like an anchor whose chain cannot withstand the fury of the wild waves. Thus, it breaks and leaves the ship defenseless. Or, to put it another way, people who base their hopes on things of the world are like the person who relies on a cane made out of a reed. The reed will break, and its splinters will enter the person's flesh.

Is there, by chance, a hope, a strong anchor, that no wind or wave can destroy? Of course there is, beloved. It is neither wealth, physical strength, skill, or science. Nor is it politics, different ideologies, great people, powerful nations, or friendships and their alliances. Today's Epistle proclaims one sound, true hope. It is Christ. Christ is not found physically on earth. He is found in heaven. Whoever believes in Him has a hope that is like an anchor which is held fast and immovable from very high—from above the stars where Christ is. The believer who is held fast from there is not afraid of falling into chaos and despair. He feels Christ consoling him in his heart and supporting him during the difficult times of his life. And again, when the believer passes over the bridge of death, this hope doesn't leave him but accompanies him until the last moment. This is how the believer leaves this world, with the certain hope that up in the heavens he shall meet Christ, and he shall live forever in the world of joy and happiness.

## THE BLOOD OF CHRIST

*The blood of Christ . . . purge your conscience from dead works to serve the living God.*

—Heb. 9:14

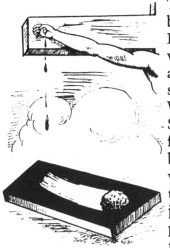

There is, beloved, a harmony between the creations of God. Let me explain. Matter, the soil we step on, is the lowest creation of God. Its purpose is to serve plants, flowers, and trees. Without it, can any plant grow? Soil, the earth, is the mother from whose entrails emerge beautiful roses, green ears of wheat, and fruit-laden trees; they are like her children. And just as the soil has as its purpose to serve the plants and trees, these things, too were created for the purpose of offering their services. And they offer them freely. For example, they serve the animals. Without grass what animal can live? Do you not see the eagerness with which the shepherd waits for the earth to grow grass so that he can lead his herd to green pastures? This grass is harvested by the animals and falls into machines that not even the smartest inventor can make. These machines which take grass and turn it into milk, fat, and meat, are the stomachs of animals. How does the grass that the animal eats become meat? It is a mystery that no scientist can explain. It is the work of God alone.

But animals were not created for themselves only. They were created to serve, too. Serve whom? Man. How difficult—let us stop short of impossible—would be the lives of people without animals. Imagine the world without animals, and you will see how difficult things would be for people. Regardless of whatever science might create as substitutes for them, their absence would be significant.

But somehow we have prolonged our discussion and we must stop. Why are we talking about farms, meadows, crops, trees, and animals today? Because we want to examine the relationship between the creations of God. We've seen, up to now, how the soil serves the plants and trees. The plants and trees serve the animals. The animals serve man. And man? Man, the finest creation of God, whom does he serve? Only himself? But then he'd be a selfish person—or, in words of the people, a lover of his own skin. Our purpose is to work and serve not only ourselves but also other people. Above all, we must serve God, thanking Him, glorifying Him, and carrying out His holy will.

To do the holy will of God! This is our purpose. Are we doing it? If we did what God wants, harmony, joy, and happiness would reign everywhere. Unfortunately, although plants and animals fulfill their purposes, man has strayed from his purpose. Instead of having God as his center, man has become his own center. Man has ignored God, despised Him, blasphemed Him, rebelled against Him, and ignored His commandments. Because of man's rejection of God, order and harmony have been disturbed.

Is man happy because of this? Hardly. There is no happiness far from God. There is only misfortune and more misfortune. Even when man has everything and seems happy externally, he's not fulfilled because he knows he is not in accord with God. He hears a voice inside him saying: "You are guilty, you have violated the moral law, you blasphemed, you have stolen, you have been dishonorable, unjust, you've killed, you've stepped upon the bodies of the dead to become rich and powerful and great." This voice can be heard inside the breast of everyone, and it leaves no one in peace. Wherever the guilty one goes—to Australia, to America, even to the moon—his inner voice will not be silent. His sins follow him. He has a burning coal inside him. Scorpions prick him. Fearsome dreams wake him. "Help," he shouts as though enemies are chasing him. He is being pursued by the wrath of God. Because of his sins, man has disturbed his harmonious relationship with God and become His enemy.

Yes, man has become God's enemy, someone worthy of hell, worthy of the punishments that the judgment of God must impose on offenders of His commandments, worthy of death. Man's guilty conscience seeks forgiveness and atonement. That's why we see that everyone prior to Christ tried to atone for their sins before God through different means. When some great calamity occurred, such as a flood, an earthquake, or an epidemic, didn't everyone believe that the wrath of God had descended upon them? By sacrificing animals, even people, they tried to appease God's wrath and stop the disasters, so that order and harmony, peace and love, would once again return to earth, representing a reconciliation between God and man.

Of all those ancient people, it was the Israelites who had the clearest idea about God before Christ. And they, like all the other people, had sacrifices—not sacrifices of people but of animals. They also had their altar, a place dedicated to God like our Holy Altar-tables. At that place, the sacrificial altar, a fire always burned. All those Jews who fell into sin would come to this sanctuary where they would offer a lamb, goat, or calf to God. The priest would slaughter the animal and burn it. He would sprinkle the sinner with the blood of the animal. The sinner would then leave in the knowledge that his sins had been forgiven.

On a certain day of the year there were prayers and sacrifices, not just for a few people but for all the people. That day was called the Day of Atonement, that is, the day on which all the sins that the people committed during the year were forgiven. They sacrificed sheep and calves on that day. The celebrant high priest would take a basin full of the blood of the animals and sprinkle all of the people with it.

For years and years the Judaic people sacrificed thousands and thousands of animals. The blood of all of these sacrifices would make an enormous river. But the Apostle Paul, in the excerpt that we've heard today, comes and shouts that all of the blood of those innumerable animals that was shed in the sanctuary of the Jews is not enough to forgive even a little sin. These sacrifices, which God had ordered, took place only as a continuous reminder that man is guilty before God and needs forgiveness. And the sacrifices were not only a continuous reminder of the sinfulness of the people but also a vivid picture of the thirst for forgiveness that the people experienced before Christ came.

Only one sacrifice saved mankind—only one blood, a blood that was pure and clean of every stain of sin. It was an immaculate blood, the blood that Christ shed on the cross. Only this blood was capable of cleansing man from his sins, of reconciling him to God, and of bringing peace, order, and harmony to the universe.

Yes, my Christians! One drop of the blood of our Lord Jesus Christ becomes a sea, an ocean. Even though they are like mountains of burning coals, the sins of the people fall into this sea and are extinguished. The sea conquers the fire. And the blood of Christ conquers every sin. Without this precious blood, who can be saved and redeemed? This we must never forget, and our gratitude to Christ must be endless.

Philippians 4:4–9

## WHERE IS THE JOY?

*Rejoice in the Lord always: and I say, Rejoice.*
—Phil. 4:4

A human being, beloved, was created for happiness. That is why God didn't drop Adam and Eve, the first people, on a desert island but put them in a fine part of the earth where there was more beauty and grace than we can imagine. This first dwelling place of man, called paradise, was an orchard filled with every blessing: pure and productive soil; clean running water, fruit-laden trees, fragrant flowers, singing birds, and tame and useful animals. The climate was perfect. A gentle wind made the treetops sway and their leaves rustle quietly, providing a pleasant, healthy breeze. There were no germs, sicknesses, or death. This was paradise.

The first human couple whom God blessed lived in paradise. God didn't ask any remuneration from them for the blessings they received. The light, the water, the fruit, the air—everything was free. God asked only one thing from them: that they obey what He commanded. God didn't ask it for Himself, because God needs absolutely nothing from people; He asked because whatever God commands is also in the best interests of man. If only man had listened to God, he would always live joyfully and happily.

Man, we know, did not obey God, choosing instead to listen to the devil when the devil hissed into his ear that he would be happy if man stopped obeying God. And man, instead of shutting his ears so as not to hear what the evil one was saying, listened to the devil's words and disobeyed God's commandment. From the moment Adam and Eve disobeyed, from that time on, happiness left and sorrow entered. Adam and Eve could not stay in paradise any longer. They left. The earth filled up with thorns. The animals became ferocious. The elements of nature revolted. The air became infected, and sickness and death appeared. These were the results of the disobedience; the results of the sin of the first people created by God.

Sorrow has reigned in the world from that time forward. The people, sorrowful, oppressed, tortured by different unhappy events, and most of all by the evil which is inside them, cannot find peace. Although they have lost paradise, they continue to look, thinking they shall find it again if they listen, not to what God is counseling them to do, but to what the devil is advising them. The devil got the first man expelled from paradise, and he continues to prevent the children of Adam and Eve from finding the true road, the narrow path that leads to the paradise of God. The devil promises happiness. He creates a false paradise by opening thousands of amusement centers all over the world. He advertises them as recreational centers, and people flock to them in hopes of finding happiness. They become tourists, traveling from city to city, spending their nights in taverns, making shameful love, playing cards, and dancing wild dances. They drink and become intoxicated. They absorb all the pleasures with all their senses. Some of the people succumb to the evil of drugs. In the beginning the drugs bring a pleasant numbness to the nerves, and the addicted people dream of fantastic worlds and are full of joy and happiness. They might even claim they are living in paradise. But alas! As soon as the influence of the drug ends, the imaginary paradise disappears, and sorrow returns more heavily. The users start to cry like little children, beating themselves and trying to commit suicide. Amusement is reduced to the death of the soul!

People, sin is worse than narcotics! If you do wrong, if you fall into sins that are shameful and unworthy of mentioning, if you satisfy sinful desires and passions, do you think you have found joy and happiness? Oh unfortunate one! You live in a fantastic and false world. Years don't pass, months, days—what am I saying—not even an hour passes until the joy you have tasted from sin becomes sadness, distress, and bitterness. Sin may be like honey in the beginning, but in the end it becomes like a poison.

Now, someone may ask, "Isn't there any happiness then?" There is happiness, my beloved. It is a happiness that all of us—men and women, young and old, poor and rich, uneducated and educated—can taste. There is joy, and if one drop of it falls into the heart of the most unfortunate person, it will make him happy. But this happiness is not found where the world is looking for it. It is not found in the sin-filled centers, in dances, in drunkenness and dissipation, in shameful sex, or in narcotics. Happiness, that is, true happiness, is found in those people who truly believe in Christ and live according to His divine commandments. Christ is the joy.

Would you like an example? It is the Apostle Paul. The apostolic excerpt, which is read today, Palm Sunday, in all of our churches, is taken from one of his letters that he sent to the Macedonians, the Philippians. Writing this Epistle, Paul is full of joy; therefore, this letter is called the Epistle of Joy. A worldly minded person reading it would think that Paul was in a happy place when he wrote it. However, how he would misjudge the situation. At the time Paul wrote the letter he was in the prisons of Rome. He was chained like a criminal for his faith in Christ, and he was waiting hour by hour for the door to open and for his persecutors to take him and execute him, as indeed they did. He was near the mouth of the beast. And though he found himself in this situation, his heart was full of joy and exultation, because he had Christ inside him. Prison was a paradise for Paul. He rejoiced because he was suffering for Christ. And he wanted to communicate this joy to all those who believe in Him, to all people. Don't you hear what he says? "Rejoice in the Lord always; and again I say, rejoice." Was such preaching of joy ever heard in the world before?

And while Paul was rejoicing in prison, not far from his jail were the palaces of Nero, the king who persecuted Paul and all the Christians. Anyone who saw these palaces would think that the person who lived in them and enjoyed all those pleasures would be fortunate and happy. But was Nero happy? No. He was an unbeliever, and corrupt as he was, he lived an unhappy life. In the end he was miserable.

What strange things! Palaces, hell; jail, paradise! It depends on the person whether a palace is hell, or a jail, paradise.

People! Those of you who want joy, imitate Paul. Believe in Christ. Love Christ. Obey Christ. And then no matter how many sorrows and misfortunes or illnesses and deaths find you, you will have a fountain from which you will drink immortal water. Your hearts will be refreshed, and you will rejoice. Yes, the fountain of joy is Christ! Drinking from it, you will invite the world, which doesn't know what joy means, to come to it and drink, and to also taste joy, real joy. You will also become a fountain of joy, and you will say, like Paul: "Rejoice in the Lord always; and again I say, rejoice."

## EASTER SUNDAY
Acts of the Apostles 1:1–8

# WORKS!

*The former treatise have I made, O Theophilus, of all
that Jesus began both to do and teach.*

—Acts 1:1

Christ, beloved, the founder of our holy Church, was a teacher. He taught things that no one before Him had ever taught, and you can be sure that no one, no matter how wise he may be, will ever say greater things than those which Christ has preached. His teaching was the highest of all teaching. There is none higher. Those who read the Bible without prejudice will tell you that of all the other teachings heard both in ancient times and today, no matter how they may dazzle people, none can compare to the teachings of Christ and all are far below that very pinnacle of Christ's divine teaching. You, too, beloved, open your Bible and read just one page, any page. Wherever you open the Bible, you will see that a river of pure gold runs before you.

Read, for example, the parable of the prodigal son (Luke 15:11-32). Read it carefully, and you will be convinced how right the philosopher was who said that if Christ had but told this one parable only, it would have been enough to prove that He was not a man but God. God, who created man, knows man's heart, knows how he thinks and acts. Because of this, the teaching of Christ, in spite of the severity which it seems to have, corresponds to the noblest of desires and aspirations of man and offers to suffering humanity what all the philosophies of the world cannot offer. Christ's teaching offers joy and peace and comfort of the heart and mind.

The greatest teaching of Christ is love, a word that was totally unknown to the ancients. Oh love, divine gift, angel with golden wings! Oh love, divine flame, the flame that Christ ignited in the hearts of people! Oh love that rises upward and reaches the stars, surpasses them, and touches God to sing hallelujah. It comes downward to embrace all of God's creatures, especially man, and creates sacred bonds of family, of brotherhood! The God-man taught love for God and love for fellow man. And in that love He enclosed all of the commandments.

Christ taught love. He taught that we should love God, the Heavenly Father. He taught that we should love our parents. He taught that we should love other people like brothers. He taught that we should love even those who are our enemies and pray for them.

But Christ did more than teach this greatest teaching. His teaching isn't the only miracle; His life is a much greater miracle. For someone to teach is an easy thing to do. But to practice what he teaches is far more difficult. Christ practiced what He taught. Christ taught that we should love God. But who loved God the Heavenly Father the way Christ did? Who ever prayed to God with the fervor Christ prayed to Him? Christ spent nights without sleep in ardent conversation with His Heavenly Father. Christ taught that we should love our parents. And He Himself, while nailed to the cross, did not forget His Holy Mother; He took care of her. Christ taught that we should love our enemies. He Himself loved His enemies, even though they hated Him with a passion.

Christ taught that we should forgive our enemies and pray for them. He prayed for and forgave His own enemies. "Father, forgive them; for they know not what they are doing," He was heard saying a few moments before He gave up His spirit to the Heavenly Father.

We must follow Christ's example. We must also do what He taught and practiced. But how, many will ask us, can we practice what Christ taught? Christ practiced these virtues, but after all He was a man and a God, and as God-man He had the strength to carry out the most difficult commandments and to accomplish the greatest works. And we're not Gods. We're people—people with weaknesses, people with faults and vices, people who want what's good, people who marvel at what Christ said—how can we do it? The morality that He taught is impossible to practice. His teaching isn't applicable, especially in present times. So what do we do?

Most of us ask this. But what do you say, Oh people? That Christ's teaching isn't feasible, is unrealizable? But if history presents you with people who also had imperfections and shortcomings but practiced the teaching of Christ, what would you say? If only one person in the world who practiced Christ's teaching were found, he would be enough to prove that Christ's teaching can be practiced. But there is not just one person who did this. Many people heard Christ's words and then did wonderful and marvelous deeds. And those who saw them marveled and said that if a religion gives such power to people to overcome weaknesses and passions and to surpass human standards, then this is a religion that is divine in origin, and He Who established it is God.

Do you want to see people who believed in Christ and did everything He taught, beloved? Open that book of the New Testament that is called the Acts of the Apostles. Today, on this holy day, this great holy day of Christianity, the Sunday of Easter, we read the beginning of the Gospel according to John, and the Epistle reading is the beginning of the Acts of the Apostles in the Divine Liturgy. The Bible is the story of the life of Christ. The Acts, a continuation of the Bible, is the story of the Apostles of Christ and the first Christians. It contains not only their teachings but also what they did. The Apostles applied Christ's teaching. They loved God, and they loved their neighbor. For this love they abandoned everything. Poorly clothed and hungry, they traveled the world, preaching everywhere and performing miracles. In some instances—don't be surprised—they performed miracles that were even greater than those of Christ. They performed them with His power and in this way proved that what He said was true when He said that "not only that which I do you shall do, but even greater things." (John 14: 12)

My beloved! We must put Christ's words, which we hear in church, into practice and into works in the community in which we live. We must show our children and future generations that faith is not dead in our times but alive—a faith that shines like the sun, shining with the brilliant teaching of Christ. It shines even more so with good deeds, with the marvelous works of men and women, of clerics and laity. Therefore, let us all go forward, beloved, to do good works, Christian works, like the ones of the first Christians, like the works of the Apostles, like the works of Christ. "Both to do and to teach."

## PREACHING WILL NOT STOP

*Go, stand and speak in the temple to the people all the words of this life.*

—Acts 5:20

Who should expect it, beloved? People who were uneducated and who didn't attend schools and universities—people to whom the world paid no attention—how does it happen that these people, poor and powerless, the Apostles, who hid in fear on Holy Friday and didn't dare come out to visit the tomb of Christ, now appeared in public and preached Christ with power? How did the timid become brave and fearless? How these illiterate people become orators and wise men? How did this change take place? It cannot be explained unless we accept the fact that two great happenings affected their lives. One was the resurrection of Christ; the other was the descent of the Holy Spirit. The Apostles saw Christ, Who arose from the grave, with their own eyes. They believed in Christ absolutely. There was no doubt whatsoever in their souls. Then, in fulfillment of Christ's promise, they received "power from on high," or the Holy Spirit, and the rabbits became lions. "Such is the change at the right hand of God."

We see today in the excerpt that was read how successfully the Apostles preached the Gospel of Christ. The Gospel has never had as much success as it had during the days of the Apostles. Don't you see? Those base and unbelieving people—the people who hated Christ and who got together on Holy Friday and shouted: "Crucify, crucify him"—they heard the Apostles who were preaching; they repented and were baptized by the hundreds and thousands.

The growth of the first Church is another miraculous event. To what, we wonder, is the astonishing growth of the first Church attributed? Why, beloved, it is attributed to the preaching of the Apostles, the preaching that came out of their mouths like fire, illuminating and warming frozen hearts. Those who heard them understood that the Apostles believed what they preached and were ready to shed their last drop of blood for Christ. Without the Apostle's preaching, would the Church have grown? Preaching is the life of the Church— not just any kind of preaching but the kind of preaching that the true preachers of the Gospel, people who believe and are ready to make every sacrifice, do.

So now we know that the major reason that the first Church was able to progress and grow was the preaching of the Apostles. But something else contributed to the growth and progress of the Church, and that was the miracles of the Apostles. As today's Epistle lesson says, "By the hands of the Apostles were many signs and wonders wrought among the people." (Acts 5:12) What miracles? Wherever the Apostles happened to pass in Jerusalem, the people brought the sick in their beds and waited in the streets and squares of the city. They waited for the Apostles to pass. The Apostles had so much power to cure the sick that it was only enough for Peter's shadow to fall on them and they became well. Even the sick who came from the neighboring cities and villages, and even those possessed by demons, were cured by the miraculous power of the Apostles. Thus the preaching of the Apostles, in combination with the miracles they performed, took on an unprecedented brilliance and made the people believe and repent. Oh, if only today's preachers had the power to perform miracles!

The progress of the Gospel and the rapid expansion of the Church did cause considerable anxiety. The Jewish authorities certainly were not pleased. They had killed Christ, thinking that by doing so the troublesome preaching would stop. But after Christ's death, the preaching did not stop, but rather continued with great success. The Jewish authorities did not expect this, and they became enraged. They arrested the Apostles and threw them in jail. They thought this action would silence the name of Christ. But again they were mistaken. A new miracle took place: God intervened. An angel unlocked the door of the jail at night and told the Apostles: "Go, stand and speak in the temple to the people all the words of this life." That is to say, the angel told them: "Go and stand there where you preached. Stand fearlessly and courageously and preach the words that bring life to dead souls. Preach to the people." Yes, to the people, the angel emphasizes, which means that, if the leaders who have the power and are full of egotism and pride don't want to hear the preaching, don't be influenced by their denial or be afraid of their persecutions. Talk to the people, women and men, young people and children. There are people out there who are not egotistical and who want to hear the preaching. The preaching of Christ, which is greater than all the preaching of the world, can't help but motivate people who are tired of hearing the dull preaching of the scribes, Pharisees, and Sadducees.

Go, stand and speak in the temple to the people all the words of this life." This voice of the angel crosses the centuries and reaches us. It is also directed to today's preachers and apostles of Christ because preaching can never stop. No one can stop it, just as no one can stop the rushing waters of a river with fences. The river will knock the fences down and continue on its way. The purpose of the river is to run. The word of God also has as its purpose to run. Yes, the word of God will run; it will be preached in all times and in all centuries. It will bring divine blessings everywhere, and it will perform the greatest of miracles. Spiritually uncultivated and waterless places will change into exceptional gardens of God's grace.

Oh bishops, priests, theologians, and preachers of Orthodoxy: listen to the voice of the angel and with heroic conviction preach the Gospel to our people.

# WHOM DO YOU WANT TO PLEASE?

*And because he [Herod] saw it pleased the Jews, he
proceeded further to take Peter also.*

—Acts 12:3

Do you remember Herod, beloved? He is that evil king
who ordered all of the infants in the vicinity of Bethlehem to be killed, with the hope that the Divine Infant,
Jesus Christ, would be among them. The killing was
terrible. Though thousands of mothers lamented, the
heart of that evil king was not moved. He was a cruel
man, full of evil and hatred. He had committed many
crimes. His end was a miserable one. His body filled up
with worms; it rotted, stank, and died. And that was how
his black soul went to hell.

Herod left behind many children and grandchildren, almost every one of whom had inherited his evil
ways. Herod was called the Great—not for the good that
he did but for the evil and destruction. Out of fear, the
people gave him the title "great." And that's how it
happens many times: criminals who devastate kingdoms
are called great and famous by the people.

One of the grandchildren of this evil king was the
Herod mentioned in today's Epistle reading. This grandchild, who had the same name as his grandfather, was
called Herod Antipas the First to differentiate him from
his grandfather Herod. He was also evil, an untamed
animal. Tainted blood, the polluted blood of his family,
ran through his veins. He had inherited the evils and
passions of his father and grandfather. He was a child and
a grandchild who had come out of the womb of a snake.

As though the evil of his corrupted progenitors was not enough, Herod Antipas increased it by associating with other evil and corrupt people.

Herod left his homeland as a young man and went to Rome, which was the first city of the world at that time. Rome was not only first in wealth and in glory but also in depravity. Herod associated with evil people, and lived for some time in the palace of Caligula, who was one of the most depraved and evil kings of the world. There he learned new lessons in evil and corruption before returning to his own country and becoming king in Judea. Evil were his father and mother. Evil was his education. The world in which he ruled was itself evil. It was a world, which not long before had gathered at the palaces of Pilate and Herod, his father, and shouted: "Death to Christ!" These same people who shouted, "Crucify Him," along with their children, most of them having hard and unrepentant souls, full of evil and hatred, didn't want to hear the name of Christ, and by their behavior forced their leaders into crimes and killings against the Christians.

A king of that kind of people would have to be a great and noble soul—a real hero who could stand up against those wicked people and their unlawful demands and say, "No! I'd rather fall from my position than do what you ask, to condemn and kill innocent people." But where are such great leaders? Pilate at least agonized over the innocence of Christ, even though in the end he retreated before the pressures brought on him by the abominable shouts of the crowd and didn't do that which his conscience told him. Instead he did what the crowd wanted. He authorized the condemnation of Christ to death. If Pilate gave in, wouldn't Herod, the grandson of a blood-thirsty king, give in?

Today's Epistle talks of the younger Herod continuing the evil activity of his forbearers. In addition to continuing the uncountable killings that the family of the Herods had committed, the younger Herod ordered the execution of an innocent man and the arrest of another innocent man. And who were these two innocent men against whom Herod's madness was directed? They were two of the finest people that humanity ever gave birth to. They were disciples of Christ, from the most select and beloved of His disciples. One was James, the brother of Christ's beloved disciple John; James and John were the children of Zebedee the fisherman, a fine father. The other was Peter. Herod killed James, and then he jailed Peter with the idea of killing him after a certain holiday.

And what was the reason? There was only one: it was the hatred that Herod cultivated against Christ and His followers. Herod couldn't stand to hear those two disciples preaching the name of Christ with such wisdom and power and attracting so many people to the new faith. The only way he could close their mouths was to kill them. So Herod, like a butcher, grabbed that blessed lamb of Christ, James, and slaughtered him with a knife. Gone was a flaming preacher of the Bible! An innocent man was killed!

Was there any protest? Did anyone go to Herod's palace and say: "O king, why are you jailing and killing innocent people? God is watching! You will be punished! He will destroy your kingdom and you will meet a bad end like your grandfather." If such brave voices were heard, perhaps Herod would have hesitated before committing the crime. Unfortunately, no voices were raised in protest from that unbelieving and depraved people. On the contrary, the Jews praised and applauded

Herod's actions. That is just what happens in turbulent times when unbelieving and depraved people rule. Crimes and killings are praised and applauded, and innocent people are condemned.

People who praise and applaud evil instead of condemning it have to be considered in some way accomplices to the crimes that take place here on earth.

This guilt of the world is emphasized in today's Epistle reading, which describes how the unjust death that Herod committed was pleasing to the Jews. Herod, upon seeing that the killing of these innocent people would make him a popular king, ordered the arrest of Peter, who was saved at the last moment by a miracle that God performed.

Oh, how most of us, too, resemble Herod, who, in order to be liked by a faithless and depraved people, committed murders! As for today's people, if we don't kill and commit crimes like Herod, we do a thousand and one other senseless, harmful, and, in many instances, sinful things, the only reason being so we can be liked by the world. Unfortunately, most of us don't pay any attention when our conscience tells us to do what God wants. But we pay attention to what most people like, and what they like, we do. There would be much less evil in the world if people didn't suffer from this psychological illness of wanting to be liked by everyone. If more people had the courage to say "no" to an unfaithful and depraved world and to go against it, the situation would be much improved. Our motto should be: Do not what pleases the world but that which pleases Christ.

# SUNDAY OF THE PARALYTIC
Acts of the Apostles 9:32–42

# DORCAS

*Now there was at Joppa a certain disciple named Tabitha, which interpretation is called Dorcas: this woman was full of good works and alms deeds which she did.*

—Acts 9:36

Dorcas! What is it? It is an animal that is well known to the people of the forests; they call it the gazelle. Now, with the passing of time, the deer have become scarce and are in danger of extinction, as are many other animals on earth. Civilization has exterminated many animals and plants by filling up the world with houses, apartment buildings, factories, and other enormous technological works which don't allow enough space for animals to live and thrive. And thus a time will come when gazelle, deer, and other such animals will only be seen in zoos.

The gazelle is one of the most beautiful animals. It is agile, runs fast, and lives in thick forests. The people of Palestine were very fond of the gazelle. The ancient Judeans liked the animal very much and often gave its name to their children. In Greek, as we said, the gazelle is called *dorcas*. In Hebrew, it is called *tabitha*.

One fine girl who lived in a Judean city then called Joppa (today's Jaffa), a harbor of the Hebrew nation, had this name. Dorcas, the young girl of Joppa, was a much-loved person in her community. She was not the daughter of some rich or prominent family; no, she was a poor girl, a seamstress who lived by her needle. But this poor girl was a noble human being who held a spiritual treasure in her heart. That spiritual treasure, which has nothing to do with worldly treasures, was her virtues. From the moment she believed in Christ, was baptized, and became a Christian, Dorcas proved that she didn't simply want to be called a Christian but wanted to live according to the commandments of the Bible. The most important commandment that Christ brought to the world is the commandment of love: "Love one another." In her life, Dorcas applied this commandment to an absolute degree.

Dorcas wasn't rich; she didn't have money enough to give alms to the poor. Many think that only the rich can give alms. "What can we give?" they say. "We need to be helped, not help others." However, Dorcas, this fine girl from Joppa, teaches us all that those who have love in their hearts can do a lot for others, even if they don't have money. Dorcas, as today's Epistle reading tells us, offered her professional abilities as a seamstress to the poor. She sewed clothes for orphans and widows for nothing. She performed many other kindnesses as well, which the Acts of the Apostles does not specifically mention but only says: "This woman was full of good works and alms deeds which she did." Dorcas wasn't, as they say, an empty glass but a glass full of the refreshing water of love. With it she watered and refreshed people who were thirsty for love, for help, and for benevolence. Dorcas was full of works of love and charity. What a blessed girl! While rich women and girls who lived in Joppa spent their time in vain amusements, paying absolutely no attention to the poor, the orphans, and the widows, Dorcas had become a fountain of love—a fountain that flowed and gave charity to the world in spite of her poverty. When she became sick and died, all the poor, all the orphans, and all the widows who had found consolation and protection near her mourned. She had been an affectionate mother to this suffering world.

Why should such a person die, some might ask? Why did God take her so soon? She should live to do good. Certainly God knows what He's doing, but when people lose someone close to them, they often are not themselves; out of sorrow they say things they shouldn't say. If we love someone, the heavenly Father loves them that much more and knows what He is doing. Only unbelievers and atheists cannot comprehend anything related to the mystery of death. That is why they cry inconsolably and criticize and blaspheme God. The Christians of Joppa, the orphans and widows that Dorcas cared for, weren't that kind of people. They believed that whatever God does is done for the best. They were only expressing with tears the pain they felt at her death. They didn't want Dorcas to die but to live many more years and to be with them. That is why, as soon as Dorcas fell sick and they saw that day by day the illness was becoming worse and she was in danger of dying, they sent for the Apostle Peter, who was at a nearby city. But by the time Peter arrived, Dorcas had died. Seeing the sorrow Dorcas's death brought on, Peter kneeled, prayed, and then said to the dead girl, "Tabitha, arise," and the miracle happened. The dead girl opened her eyes, sat up, and started speaking! The miracle became known throughout the whole district immediately, and the people believed in Christ.

Dorcas, this exemplary girl from Joppa, teaches us a lot. But in this short sermon of mine I want you to pay close attention to a detail—the name of this fine girl. She was called Dorcas, and she proved herself to be a Dorcas. That is to say, just as the gazelle is an agile animal that runs everywhere and traverses great distances until it finds pure water, in the same way this daughter of Joppa ran and did not rest until she drank the water and was refreshed, or, to put it another way, until she could do good to other people. Doing good to others was like being refreshed herself. And just as the gazelle looks to the left and to the right so as not to fall into the trap of the hunters, this daughter of Joppa did the same thing. She was a very careful disciple of Christ. Spreading good works both to the left and to the right, she was careful not to fall into the traps of the Devil; she kept her body clean and free from the sins of pride and vanity. Thus she lived up to the name that had been given to her. She was Dorcas not only in name but also in deed.

We, beloved, have names greater than the name that this noble young woman of Joppa had. We have Christian names, names that the saints had, these great heroes of our Orthodox faith. These names were given to us at the time we were baptized to remind us always that we must live as the saints did. What a shame to live contrary to the lives of those saints whose names we have. It is like insulting them and dishonoring their sacred memories. Even worse is to blaspheme and dishonor another name, which is above all other names——the name Christian. Our names call to us: Oh Greek Christians, either change your name or change your behavior.

May all of us who have Christian names realize our responsibility and live a perfect Christian life in accordance with the Bible so that there may be harmony between our names and our lives.

# SUNDAY OF THE SAMARITAN WOMAN
Acts of the Apostles 11:19–30

## UNTIL THE END

*And exhorted them all, that with purpose of heart they would cleave unto the Lord.*

—Acts 11:23

The first persecution began, beloved. It was preached in the capital of Israel, Jerusalem. When the leaders of the Jews—the high priests, scribes, and Pharisees—heard that Christ had risen from the grave, they began preaching a persecution of His disciples and Apostles, who were preaching His resurrection. The idea that He Whom they had crucified had risen from the grave and would come again to judge the world—that idea alone —had shaken the authorities. The wretches thought that they wouldn't be safe until the news about Christ's being resurrected was suppressed. Therefore, they conducted a persecution of the Church and the preachers of the Bible. Stephen was the first victim of this persecution.

Stephen was one of the first seven deacons the Church selected to serve the material needs of the believers: None of the Christians was supposed to go hungry. Stephen emerged as an affectionate father of the people. He took care of not only the material but also the spiritual needs of the people who believed in God. He treated everyone fairly and with love. He preached the word of God with a burning heart, and his example brought many people to the new faith. It was Stephen's success in winning converts to the Church that brought on the anger of the unbelieving Jews. Stephen, this fiery preacher of the Bible, had to be exterminated by any means, they decided. They arrested him, judged him, condemned him, and took him out of the city, where thousands of fanatical Jews stoned him. The whole time Stephen kneeled, imitating Christ in all things and praying for his murderers.

The unbelievers hoped that the preaching would stop after Stephen's execution. But not only did it not stop; it spread even more. Prior to Stephen's martyred death the preaching was confined to the city of Jerusalem; now it spread beyond the city. Christians who were forced to leave Jerusalem because of the persecution scattered to all parts, reaching places as far as Phoenicia, Cyprus, and Antioch. They preached the Gospel of Christ everywhere. Instead of suppressing christianity as the Jews expected, the persecution helped spread the Gospel outside of Jerusalem. This is how it always happens: As much as the religion of Christ is beaten, it grows and roots itself more deeply into the hearts of people. Wherever a Christian is martyred for his or her faith, God raises others to continue the fervent preaching of the Gospel.

Antioch, in particular, was where the preaching had exceptional success. This city was one of the largest in the ancient world. At that time, Antioch had a population of about half a million people. Some Christians came to Antioch from Cyprus and Libya, coastal districts of Egypt. They preached Christ in that great city. Their names? The Acts of the Apostles in the Holy Bible doesn't mention them. They were simple people, humble and unsophisticated, like the first disciples of Christ. But what did this matter? The flame of faith and love for Him burned in their hearts. And they didn't hide what they believed. They preached it to others, and their simple but faith-filled words brought marvelous results. People who lived in the darkness of sin saw the truth and believed in Christ. In this way a Church with many believers was established in Antioch.

The news that the preaching of the Gospel had progressed so much in this large city of Antioch was heard with special gladness by the faithful in Jerusalem. The Apostles decided that it would be good to send Barnabas, an important preacher of the Bible, to Antioch. Barnabas went there and started to preach—a preaching that made a special impression on the people. The grace of God shone on his face; he was what he said. Whoever heard him couldn't separate his words from his life. He was a living icon of Christ. Barnabas's preaching contributed greatly to the growth and strengthening of the Church of Antioch. And when Barnabas saw that he alone was unable to instruct and teach that many people, he searched for and found a co-worker. He found Paul, who was living in Tarsus and hadn't as yet appeared publicly to preach. Barnabas brought Paul to Antioch, and from the day Paul arrived, he started to preach. New, astonishing progress was noticed in the Church. Besides the other great and glorious things that took place with Paul's coming, those who believed in Christ were called Christians. And from that time, those people who believed in Christ have been known by this name.

From the apostolic excerpt that was heard today, I would ask you to keep one admonition that Barnabas addressed to the first Christians at Antioch as a lesson to us, too. He admonished them, it says, to remain dedicated to our Lord Jesus Christ. Yes! To remain dedicated to

Him with all of their hearts, till the end. Barnabas made this exhortation because he knew that many people listen to a sermon and believe in Christ, but they don't all stay faithful until the end. In the beginning they walk God's road willingly, but as soon as the first obstacles appear, they get discouraged, and return to their old, sinful ways. They are not firm and unshakable in their decisions. And so, out of a hundred people who believe and follow Christ, at the end of the road only a few remain—very few, two, three, or perhaps four or five. The others? They become deserters, traitors, and Christ's enemies.

Because of this, my beloved, let's pay attention to this admonition of the Apostle Barnabas. Let us pray to the Lord, not just today and tomorrow, but at all times until our very last breath, that we may remain close to Him, as His faithful and dedicated children, as true Christians, as were those first Christians who believed and became martyrs for Him.

## SUNDAY OF THE BLIND MAN
Acts of the Apostles 16:16–34

# NO ONE TO THE FORTUNE TELLERS

*And it came to pass, as we went to prayer, a certain damsel possessed with a spirit of divination met us, which brought her masters much gain by soothsaying.*
—Acts 16:16

Beloved, near-present day Kavala there was an ancient city called Philippi. Today, only its ruins remind one of its ancient glory and might. The Apostle Paul came to this city with his co-worker Silas to preach Christ. They were the first to set foot in Macedonia for this purpose. All of Macedonia at that time—in fact, all of Greece, all of the Balkans, all of Europe, from one end to the other, was idolatrous. Everyone worshiped idols, those false gods that have the devil behind them.

Idolatry was at its essence demon worship. The instruments of this demon worship were sorcerers, and sorcery spread everywhere. There wasn't a city or a village that didn't have a sorcerer. Anyone who had someone sick at home, who wanted to know what would happen in the future, or who wanted to avenge an enemy went to the sorcerers. The sorcerers, by opening certain magical books and saying words that no one understood, created the impression that the particular problem would be taken care of. Those who fell into the clutches of the sorcerers paid dearly.

There were also official centers of this satanic profession called mantic shrines. The sorcerers and sorceresses boasted that from these shrines they communicated with the gods, especially with the god Apollo, who inspired them to predict the future. The notorious oracle of ancient times was Pythia, who lived in the oracular center of Delphi.

In the great city of Philippi, there was an oracle who was a slave girl. Her masters had bought her at the slave market and exploited her. Whatever money she received from foolish people who came to hear her she gave to her masters, who divided it among themselves. Others sell the flesh of unfortunate women, but these masters of Philippi exploited this satanic profession of their slave to make money. Oh, what exploitation there is in this world! How unfortunate when such women fall into the hands of unscrupulous people and have to work like slaves at the most shameful, dishonorable, and satanic work.

The oracle of Philippi closed her mouth a few days after Paul and Silas came to the city. She could no longer predict the future. The satanic fountain that had run for many years in that city, filling the pockets of those skillful exploiters with money, stopped running. How did it stop? The power of Christ stopped it. The Apostle Paul stopped it. When the oracle of Philippi saw the Apostles, she realized that they had come to end the darkness and bring the light of Christ, to abolish the nation of the devil, and to establish the Kingdom of Christ. Should she challenge the enormous power of Christ? Satan, realizing that he would be defeated anyway, told the oracle to behave differently, to use deception, a means sorcerers and sorceresses use to this day. While they serve the devil to deceive naive people, they pretend to practice some holy rites. They carry icons, burn incense, and light candles. In this way, using these organs of the devil, they are pretending to be using organs of God to love and protect the religion. The oracle of Philippi was one who used this deceptive method. Whenever she saw the

Apostles, she came out into the streets and shouted: "Do you see those people? They are servants of God the Most High. They came to show us the true road, the road of salvation."

Paul didn't want to be acknowledged by a seeress who served the devil. He was in a position to understand what Satan was trying to do by advocating the Bible through the oracle. Satan wanted to mix things up and bring about confusion. Paul wanted things to be clear and delineated. Here is the light; there is darkness. Here is the truth; there is the lie. Here is Christ; there is the devil. He wanted no friendship, alliance, or endorsement from Satan. An open war with Satan would have been preferable to a peace that betrayed the faith and disguised the truth. Frank language is always preferable; the condemnation of a faithless and wicked world must always be heard strongly, continuously, and unceasingly. This is what Paul did. Full of indignation against that deceiving oracle who was commending him and his preaching, Paul walked up to her and said: "Wicked spirit, in the name of Jesus Christ I order you to come out." The evil spirit came out of the slave girl as soon as Paul said these words, and that satanic fountain that had been poisoning so many souls, the fountain of the oracle, dried up forever. Joy to the faithful. Joy to the angels and archangels. Joy to Christ. But sorrow for the devil, and sorrow for the devil's instruments, because the money stopped falling into the purses of the exploiters.

The masters of the seeress, who saw their commerce in sorcery being destroyed and their clientele and great profits being lost, became enraged at Paul. They hated the Apostle like the deadly enemy of their interests that he was. They went to the authorities of the city and accused Paul and Silas of being dangerous people, of being overthrowers of the political and religious establishment. As a result, the Apostles were arrested. They were brutally beaten by the Roman soldiers and thrown into the jail at Philippi. Whoever sees the ruins of this jail has to be moved, because it bears witness to the miracle that God performed to free His faithful servants.

Twenty centuries have passed since that time, beloved, and sorcery still hasn't disappeared. In an age, particularly like the one we live in now, when the people have drifted far away from Christ's faith, we would expect them to fall victim to sorcery. Sorcerers and sorceresses, unfortunately, are not only in our villages but also in our big cities. The young and the old, the uneducated and educated, run to them to ask about their fortunes. Recently, astrologists, themselves nothing more than sorcerers who try to foresee the future from the signs of the zodiac and from the movement of the stars, have appeared in the big cities. One family told me how upset they were to have found talismen in their yard. They were afraid that something evil would happen to them. But the true Christian who believes just as Paul and the other Apostles believed, is not afraid of sorcerers. The true Christian knows that Christ defeated the demons. Every believer will receive the strength to defeat sorcerers and sorceresses, and all of Satan's minions. For when they hear the name of Christ, those satanic followers tremble and go far from the person who believes in Christ and lives and behaves according to His holy will.

## STS. CONSTANTINE AND HELEN
Acts of the Apostles 26:1, 12–20

# A MIRACLE

*Saul, Saul, why are you persecuting me It hurts you*
*to kick against the goads.*
—Acts 26:14 NRSV

There are, beloved, people who doubt that our religion is true. They doubt that Christ is the true God Who was crucified, resurrected, and ascended to the heavens where He continues to live and reign. They doubt the Church that Christ established. They doubt His teaching. They doubt everything that is related to Him and His holy Church. In order to believe, they say, they want proof. They want miracles.

To those who doubt, one could cite many proofs and arguments. One could even relate older and recent miracles that took place in the name of Christ. But we will bypass these and mention only one miracle, which is enough to convince any well-intentioned person that our religion is true. This miracle is Paul. He is enough to prove that Christ is the only true God Who lives and reigns. Now I ask you, what was Paul before he believed in Christ He was, as he himself confesses, a fanatic Jew. He was convinced that the Messiah for whom he awaited was an all-powerful king who would crush all the kingdoms of the world and establish a vast Judaic empire. Because of this belief, Paul could not believe that Christ, Who died on the cross, could be the true Messiah. Paul believed that everything concerning Christ was a great error that threatened to spread and destroy the Jewish nation. For this reason he hated Christ. Just hearing Christ's name and would make him very angry. Whenever Paul heard that there were Christians somewhere, he would capture them and throw them into prison. He himself struck many of them. He was always present at the court hearings against them, and if he heard that the verdict was "Death to the Christians," he would applaud with pleasure. He was especially happy when he could coerce Christians into blaspheming Christ. The hatred that nested inside him turned Paul into such a maniac that while he was angry or filled with vengeance, he was beside himself and didn't know what he was doing. He hunted Christians inside Jerusalem. He would go to other cities and villages of Judea, and even beyond Judea, to persecute them. His name was synonymous with fear and terror. He was Saul (as Paul was called before he believed in Christ).

Who would have expected that this persecutor of Christians would become a worshiper and preacher of the crucified One? Yet Paul became such. And how? He narrates it himself in the apology he makes before King Agrippa:

> I received orders from the high priests of the Jews to go to a far city, Damascus, to persecute the Christians. With me were others. We were walking. But while we were walking on the road to Damascus and it was noontime and the sun shown in the sky, suddenly I saw a light coming from the sky that was far brighter than the light of the sun, shining around me and those who were with me. We couldn't face that bright light and we fell down. And while all were down, I heard a voice talking to me in Hebrew and saying: "Saul, Saul, why are you persecuting me? It is hard for you

to kick against the goads." I said to him: "Who are you, Lord?" And he answered: "I am Jesus, the one you persecute. But arise, stand on your feet. For I have appeared to you for this purpose, to make you a minister and a witness both of these things which you have seen, and of those things in which I will appear to you; delivering you from the people, and from the Gentiles, to whom now I send you, to open their eyes, and to turn them from darkness to light, and from the power of Satan to God, that they may receive forgiveness of sins, and inheritance among them that are sanctified by faith in me."

That's what I say, that's what I heard, O King. To this heavenly vision I could not be disobedient. I started to preach Christ in every land. My preaching is that people should repent and believe in Christ and do works of penance.

Paul changed completely from the time he saw that light and heard Christ's voice. He saw Christ, Whom he thought was dead, alive before him with indescribable brightness and power. He saw Him reproving him and talking to him. After this vision, he had no further doubts that Christ was the true God, the God Who governs heaven and earth, and from inexpressible condescension toward a sinful mankind came to earth to call people to repentance. Paul saw, he heard, and he believed. And his faith became like an unshakable rock, which no temptation could dislodge. From that time on, whoever heard Paul speaking about Christ was convinced that Paul was not lying. Whoever reads Paul's epistles today must be convinced that a rare and unique witness——a witness who with absolute honesty hides nothing but publicly confesses his great sins and asks mercy—is present. Paul glorifies and thanks God that the mercy that he asked for he found in the cross, in the bloody hands and feet of Christ. He falls and worships his benefactor. Christ, I thank you.

Paul preaches Christ. And if we don't believe in Paul, in whom, I beg you, shall we believe?

Paul saw the light. But what was this light? Was it light like the lights that people turn on at night? Was it light like the light that shines from the stars, and even more so, the sun? No. The light that Paul saw had no resemblance either to artificial lights or the natural light of the stars and sun. It was a special light—a light above all lights, a light outshining the sun itself during that moment of its greatest brightness, a light that made the sun and all of the stars go out. It was a supernatural light, a light that comes from the never-setting light. And that never-setting light of the world is Christ.

"Come and receive the light from the never-setting light," as Paul received it and lit his torch, made it a sun, and brought this light to the whole world.

Unbelievers try to give another explanation for Paul's conversion, but their efforts are in vain. No other interpretation can stand. What happened on the road to Damascus is a fact—a fact more certain than the sun high up in the sky. Paul saw a vision and believed. Paul is a miracle—one of the greatest miracles—that proves that Christ is He Who creates such great, unimaginable changes in the hearts of people and to Whom belongs the power, the honor, and the glory forever.

# PENTECOST

*And when the day of Pentecost was fully come, they were all with one accord in one place.*

—Acts 2:1

Today, my beloved, is the feast of Pentecost. Pentecost—a great feast that the Christians of the whole world celebrate. The Hebrews also celebrate Pentecost. But what a difference between the one and the other, our Pentecost from the Pentecost of the Hebrews! It differs like the sun from a star at night, like a person from his shadow. The Pentecost of the Hebrews is a shadow—a shadow that shows reality. And that reality is the Pentecost that the Christians celebrate today.

But let us describe with a few words the Pentecost of the Hebrews and the Pentecost of the Christians.

Pentecost for the Hebrews is the occasion for remembering a great happening that took place in the history of the Old Testament. All of us know from history that the Hebrews were slaves of the Egyptians. Their slavery was awful. They lived in huts. They worked from morning to night. They carried stones, baked bricks, and built palaces and tombs for their masters. They had no comforts. They had to throw their male children into the Nile as soon as they were born. The aim of the Egyptians was to exterminate them, their logic being that if children are not born or if born, are taken and killed, the people will disappear from the face of the earth. The Hebrew nation was heading toward extinction. But God had compassion and sent a great and capable leader, Moses, to liberate the people of God from the slavery of the Egyptians. After four hundred years, the Hebrews saw freedom. All of them, men, women and children, left Egypt on a great journey to their homeland, Palestine. They suffered much until they reached their beloved country. All of this is narrated in a book of the Old Testament called Exodus. I recommend it to you; you will benefit very much from it. Buy the Old Testament now it has been translated into simple language.

One of the first events that took place during the return of the Hebrews to their homeland occurred fifty days after the departure of the Hebrews from Egypt. On the top of a mountain, Sinai, God gave the Ten Commandments, the Decalogue, to His faithful servant Moses. The presentation was a significant event not only for the Hebrew people but for the whole world. A star appeared in the middle of the darkness, lighting the road people should follow if they wanted to live with justice, harmony, and love.

The Hebrews celebrate this event—the receiving of the Decalogue—on the day of Pentecost. But together with this event, the Hebrews celebrate another event that happens every year. It is the harvest. The Hebrews harvest their fields and take the first ears of wheat, thresh them, and grind them. From this new flour they make pure loaves of bread and offer them at the sanctuary. Thus they express their gratitude to God, for without His blessing, without the sun, without the rain and suitable weather, they couldn't collect even a handful of grain from the fields. "Our God! Thou Who hast blessed our crops and given us new bread, we thank Thee. Thou gave us also something more important than bread. Thou gavest us our freedom from terrible slavery. Our God, our Father, we Thy children, thank Thee." This was the prayer, this was the meaning that the feast of Pentecost had for the Hebrews.

The feast of Pentecost that the Christians celebrate today has a meaning, as we said, which is much greater than the meaning of the Pentecost of the Hebrews. Listen carefully to the reason why.

God gave to the Hebrews, through Moses, the Decalogue, the Ten Commandments, which Christ afterwards completed with His teaching. But Christ didn't only give us His perfect evangelical law that the ages marvel at; He also gave us something that Moses did not receive. Fifty days after His glorious resurrection, Christ, in accordance to the promise He had made, sent the Holy Spirit to His disciples, together with His Most Holy Mother, the myrrh-bearing women, and a few other faithful and devoted people who were gathered in a house in Jerusalem. There were 120 souls in all. These few were the first seeds that would be planted; they would multiply and become uncountable millions of Christians. The Holy spirit came to those few people in whom the whole Church, the Church of all the centuries, lay hidden. The Holy Spirit came like a strong wind. It came like fire.

What does the wind do when it is strong? It uproots trees that were planted in the earth for years. When the Holy Spirit comes to a person like a strong wind, it uproots evils and passions that are like wild trees rooted in the person's heart. And in their place it plants other trees of the virtues of Christ. And what does fire do? It illuminates, warms, and burns. The Holy Spirit illuminates the mind, warms the heart, and burns the thorns of evils and passions.

The Holy Spirit, then, gives Christians a powerful strength. With the help of the Holy Spirit, the faithful execute the commandments of Christ and do great and wondrous works. Before the Holy Spirit came, people were very weak morally. They heard the good, saw the good, admired the good, but couldn't do it. They were like the lame man who sees how beautiful a mountain-top is but cannot climb up to it to enjoy the view. They were like the sick man who wants to get well but doesn't have the  medicine that he needs to be healed. The Holy Spirit gives people the power to stand on their feet and walk steadily on God's road. It gives medicine which strengthens the will and makes it strong and indomitable. Do you want proof? The proof is the Apostles. What were they before the Holy Spirit came? And what did they become after the Holy Spirit came? We all know. The Apostles, once as timid as rabbits, became as brave and fearless as lions. Who, I ask you, gave them this power to preach the grandeur of God before thousands of people? The Holy Spirit performed this miracle.

The Hebrews, as we have seen, harvested their fields on the day of Pentecost and collected their first crops. But what is this harvest compared to what the Apostles harvested on this holy day of Pentecost? They preach and plant the word of God, and their words take root and dried-out hearts bear fruit. The valley turns green, it turns yellow. O my God, what a miracle! Three thousand souls believe on the day of Pentecost and are baptized in Christ. They are the first crop of Christianity. And I ask you now: Isn't our Pentecost countless times better than the Pentecost of the Hebrews? Theirs is a mere shadow, while ours is a reality.

## SUNDAY OF ALL SAINTS
Hebrews 11:33–40;12:1–2

# VICTORS

*Wherefore seeing we also are compassed about with so great a cloud of witnesses, let us lay aside every weight, and the sin which doth so easily beset us, and let us run with patience the race that is set before us.*

—Heb. 12:1

They won! If the people of our time who have gone crazy with ball games heard this refrain, their thoughts would immediately turn to some football game, and they would anxiously wait to hear if their team won. They won! Then they would express their happiness; they would even have a demonstration and run through the streets shouting and disturbing the whole city. What frenzy, what madness!

Not long ago on a Sunday in a small village, while the priest was ringing the bell calling the villagers to church, the people got into three buses and traveled many miles to a city to see a football match between their village's team and another team. The church was empty. There wasn't even an altarboy to hold a candle. That night, when the villagers returned, they were sad and dejected, almost crying because their team had lost. They even turned against the priest because he hadn't gone with them to bless the team. The ball game, you see, has become a god that millions of people venerate and worship. And the player with the strongest feet who gives the ball the hardest kicks is the person they honor and applaud; he is the victor.

These victories on the playing fields are small and unimportant. Nothing comes out of them. There are, however, other kinds of victories that are truly great and important; they are victories that our ancestors have noted and appreciated. The Greeks were idol worshipers. They loved athletics, and they honored the athletes—not with money the way we pay professional athletes today but with a crown of laurel. Our ancient forefathers loved athletics that exercised not just the feet but the whole body. Exercise was not just for a few people but for all of the children and youth. The idea was that they should have strong bodies to defend their country in time of war. Greek athletics are certainly worthy of emulation, at least by us Greeks. Furthermore, we should exercise according to the ancient standard rather than mimic the practices of foreign countries who have exploited athletics for commercial gain.

Even more than bodily exercises, our ancient forefathers valued something else. As a greater victory, above all the other victories, even the martial ones, they valued the victory of virtue. They had a saying: The greatest victory is to conquer yourself.

Yes, to conquer yourself! But who is that self we have to conquer? He is, as we have had the opportunity to say before, our corrupt self—our vices, our faults, our passions. Is it easy for a person to conquer himself? Let us take one from among many examples. From this example alone we will see how difficult it is.

Drinking has to be one of the most pitiful vices there is. By drinking continuously, one is in danger of becoming an alcoholic. Wine, beer, and all the other alcoholic beverages become a necessity for the alcoholic. In fact, the alcoholic could do without water before he could go without alcohol. Even if alcohol is denied him, even if all the bars and liquor stores are closed, he will find a way to get his "fix"—that is to say, to find alcohol. Almost a century ago, when the selling of alcohol was prohibited in America and those who imported it were punished severely, alcoholic beverages went on the black market. Shiploads came to America from Europe. The cursed cargo was unloaded on the seacoasts at night. If the smugglers were in danger of being caught, they would throw the cases overboard so they could be recovered later. We use this example to show that not even the money that the alcoholic wastes or the danger that alcohol poses to his health, not even the advice of his doctor or the tears of his wife and children, and not even the chains of prison can make the alcoholic hate his corrupt self and conquer his passion for drink.

The alcoholic finds himself possessed, controlled by sin. They say that Alexander the Great, who defeated all his enemies, at the end of his life became entangled with evil foreign people. He often got drunk, and one day in anger he killed his best friend. Upon sobering up in the morning, he realized what a great evil he had committed. He took out his sword and tried to kill himself. And he would have, had his aides not stopped him. What a sad thing! He who conquered the entire world was conquered by himself. He was conquered by the evil of drunkenness. Were they not right when our ancient forefathers said that the greatest victory is the victory over ourselves?

Conquer, then, your evils, your vices, and your passions. Then you will be a victor worthy to receive the garland of glory.

One might wonder if there are such victors in this world. Indeed there are. They are the spiritual heroes—the martyrs and confessors of our faith. They are the brave athletes of virtue. Let us call them by the name that our Church calls them, even if we know that this name doesn't make much of an impression on a world that kicks at God and virtue and lives like a herd of animals and wild beasts. Yes, let us call them Saints, the victors our Church celebrates and honors today.

All of the Saints are victors in the most beautiful and important contest that a person is called upon to enter in this world. The Saints are victors in the contest of faith and virtue. They defeated the greatest and most dangerous enemy, the sin that in today's apostolic reading is called "the sin that so easily entangles." Sin is like a wicked person who shows all of his or her charms and throws his or her nets everywhere to induce people to do wrong. That is why sin is called that which so easily entangles.

All of the Saints defeated sin. They were men, women, boys, girls, and even small children. They defeated sin with the weapons of light. They defeated sin by taking strength from Christ, Who was the first to defeat sin and the devil, and Who is the leader of the Christian array. Can we count these victors? They are numberless. They are a radiant cloud.

Today the Church calls us to this beautiful contest. The hearts of each of us are the vast stadium of this sacred contest. The time for the contest has come, and the opposing team, the team of the passions, has made its appearance on the field. Who makes up this team? Look! They are pride, vanity, avarice, fornication, anger, envy, greed, indolence, and carelessness. These passions carry with them many, many other evils. Go forward, then! The trumpet of the contest calls to us. Christians, fight against these passions! With the grace of God, defeat "the sin that so easily entangles," and you will be worthy of heavenly glory and joy.

# HONEY OR POISON?

*Tribulation and anguish, upon every soul of man that doeth evil. . . .*

—Rom. 2:9

Sin, we said in a previous homily, beloved, doesn't appear as it actually is. For if it did, then everyone would avoid it like the greatest danger of their lives. Sin is like an ugly and dirty person who elicits disgust and aversion. It is like the frightening beast that John saw in the Revelation; it had a body with seven heads, each one of which was trying to snatch someone to eat. The seven heads snatch their victims, and no matter which mouth devours them, the victims will go to the same stomach. The beast represents sin. The seven heads represent the seven mortal sins. The victims, of course, are people. The stomach represents hell and damnation, where all unrepentant sinners will go. In spite of this analogy, people do not avoid sin. Why? Because sin is camouflaged and appears different from what it is. Satan takes sin and dresses it up in the most beautiful clothes. He decorates it with false little stones and paints it with the most vivid colors. This way it glitters in the eyes of people and makes them think it's something very important that they have to have and enjoy.

Sin resembles a curious flower that grows in tropical lands. It is called Refreshing. In the morning it opens up its leaves. The leaves are covered with a certain sweet, sticky liquid. Small insects land on the leaves and eat this honeylike nectar. The poor things! As they sit there carelessly, the plant suddenly closes itself up, turning itself into a ball. It kills the insects and eats them. In a little while it opens up, and again its leaves gather up other insects.

Sin is like that flower. It seems sweet in the beginning. People who are caught by it think that they're happy. How beautiful, how sweet is this life, they say. They eat of the honey of sin. In a little while, however, the sin that seems so beautiful and sweet reveals itself for what it really is. It is anxiety and agony. It is corruption and destruction. It is humiliation and dishonor. It is bitter death. It is hell and damnation. It is also the young people of today, especially the young who live in the Scandinavian countries of Denmark, Sweden, and Norway. These young people have thrown away the Christian teaching about abstinence and prudence as though it were worthless. They no longer consider the dirtiest and most abominable sin evil. Young men and women sin without shame or fear of anyone, as though sin were something very natural, like drinking a glass of water.

*La dolce vita* (the sweet life) is their motto. They are like herds leaving their country and traveling to different lands to enjoy the sweet life. And the result? In the beginning life is sweet. But in the end, it proves to be a life full of bitterness and death in itself. Young as they are, in the prime of life, when they should glow with happiness and optimism, they become skeptical and melancholy after living such a prodigal and corrupt life. They don't see any meaning to life. Not wanting to live anymore, they kill themselves. The sin in which they labored and spent all of their energies has paid them dearly with death.

And it isn't just the young who sin and live a debauched life and experience how bitter it is in the end. It is everyone who sins and doesn't repent and ask God's forgiveness. They will taste the sorrow-filled results. For example, the time will come when a thief, who steals from the young and old, who breaks into houses and businesses, and who lives by his ill-gotten gains, shall pay for this sin. While robbing, he believes that no one will ever discover him, but because of some unimportant detail, the police pick up a clue, follow it, and identify the guilty party. When the thief sees the police at his door, he becomes anxious and agitated. "They've discovered me!" he says to himself. "What's going to happen to me now? Cursed is the hour I learned to steal and live from other people's sweat." In jail, where he is now going, he'll have time to think seriously about his situation; he will learn that sin, which brought him so much gain in the beginning, in the end has only led him to jail. Now he doesn't have a dollar with which to buy a loaf of bread.

Here is another sinner. He doesn't steal or break into houses and businesses; he does something worse. With lies and flattery, with promises, with satanic willes, he succeeds in convincing his neighbor's wife to commit the sin of adultery and spreads destruction and misfortune in that house. Do you think he's happy? Everything but. If you could open up his heart, you would see a scorpion is biting him and won't leave him in peace. It's the voice of his conscience. Even though it seems to be sleeping, it is awake and shouting: "You dishonorable man, you criminal, what did you do? You destroyed your neighbor's house!" And this voice won't be silenced.

But, beloved, is there any need to run to others to find out what happens in their hearts when they sin? The evidence is very close to us. We are it. Don't we sin? Whoever says that he has never sinned is lying. There isn't a person "who lives and does not sin." There is only one person who is without sin: Christ. What happens, then, inside us when we commit some sin, small or great? Have you ever seen a child who has done something wrong face his parents? He's worried and anxious. The parents realize right away that the child has done something, and because of this their sadness is painted on their faces. Only if the child confesses and the parents forgive him and show him love and compassion again, will the child find happiness. On the other hand, when a child does something good, oh then with how much joy does he run home to hear his parents congratulate and praise him?

We are children of the heavenly Father, too. When we do His holy will and do what is good, oh then what joy, what peace and happiness we experience in the depths of our hearts! On the other hand, when we go against His will and live a sinful life, then our hearts do not experience peace. We are sad and depressed and can't explain the reason for it. We have no one else but ourselves to blame for the sins we commit. Happiness has left us because we've sinned so much. And so again in our century the words of the Apostle that were heard today are proved true: "Tribulation and anguish, upon every soul of a person that doeth evil, of the Jew first, and also of the Gentile; but glory, honor, and peace, to every one that worketh good, to the Jew first, and also to the Gentile." (Rom. 2:7-10)

**THE THIRD SUNDAY OF MATTHEW**
Romans 5:1–10

## THE LOVE OF GOD

*But God commendeth his love toward us, in that, while
we were yet sinners, Christ died for us.*
—Rom. 5:8

Everyone today, beloved, speaks about love. Love is the noblest and deepest feeling God planted in the hearts of people. What if someone were to take it away from the world? Alas! The world wouldn't last; it would collapse and perish. Love is as necessary to the universe as gravity. How do the millions and billions of stars in the heavens stay there? Why don't they move out of their orbits and crash into each other? How do they move around with such harmony and grace? Who is it that controls them? It is God. God made a law, a natural law, a law that is the most important law in the universe. This law is called universal gravitation. And what does it mean It means that there is a power hidden in every planet or star that, like a magnet, pulls at other heavenly bodies that are near to it; they, in turn, pull on it, and in this way, with the one pulling at the other, they are controlled so as not to fall out of the skies. Universal gravitation is the unseen thread that holds all of the planets together. And this is certainly a great mystery. How the earth, for example, pulls at the moon, the moon pulls at the earth, and again they are pulled by the sun; the sun is pulled by another sun; and the other sun by another; and so on. An endless chain! It makes you giddy thinking about it.

Then, just as the billions of stars are controlled by the law of universal gravitation, the millions and billions of people of the world are controlled by another law, the moral law that God planted in the hearts of people. This law is the law of love.

There is not a person alive who does not feel the law of love. Even a criminal who committed awful crimes and is condemned to death—even he has something of the law of love inside him. If every vestige of love were to be extinguished, and a person felt that no one loved him and he had been abandoned, he would not be able to live; he would commit suicide.

People need love! But love for Adam and Eve, the first couple, was pure love—love free from every defilement of sin. Heaven was reflected in their eyes. It was joy and happiness. Adam loved Eve, and Eve loved Adam. The two of them loved God, Whom they felt to be like a father, above all things. There was harmony between those first two people in their relationship with nature, with each other, and with God. They, like spiritual stars, gravitated around the center, around God, and were in an orbit of divine love. Everything was wonderful.

After Adam and Eve committed sin, however, the harmony of the relationship was disturbed. Love was distorted and infected; it became a selfish love that restricted itself to a few people. It was a love that didn't have God as its center of gravitation but other centers, such as people and things. Instead of loving God, people loved only themselves and their pitiful interests. Thus instead of being lovers of God, they were lovers of sensual things, lovers of themselves, worshipers of their body, egotists all around. Their motto became: Everything for ourselves, nothing for our neighbor, nothing for God. Love became stripped of everything that was good and beautiful, and only its name remained. Oh, how many crimes have been committed in the name of this false love!

But where, you may ask, is this pure love, this ideal love? Where is this Christian love, which doesn't hold anything back for itself except the cross, instead sacrificing everything for others?

Ideal love is in God. God is love, as the evangelist John preaches (1 John 4:8). There are not just one or two examples of divine love; there are countless examples. Which one of these shall we mention in this brief homily? God provided very well for man; He put him in the middle of paradise, in a natural environment which cannot be compared with anything else in beauty. Wherever man stood, he saw beauty: in the air that was free of every germ and blew and moved the leaves of the trees; in the crystalline water that ran and murmured; in the sun's rays that shined and warmed; in the branches of the fruit-laden trees; in the birds that sang in the thick foliage; in all of the tame animals that lived lovingly together in the coenobium of paradise. Each of them was separate from the other, yet all together they called with a mystical voice, and their sweet sounds reached the ears of Adam and Eve, saying God loves you!

But God didn't stop loving man and being concerned about him after Adam and Eve's fall. Every so often He would send people who had special abilities and gifts. He sent patriarchs and prophets, and through these chosen spirits showed His love and His desire to bring His people to the knowledge of God.

Unfortunately, in spite of all that God did, in spite of all the blessings and miracles, the people were not moved and did not repent. They did not return to the heavenly Father. And God? Although He could destroy them, just as He destroyed Sodom and Gomorrah, He didn't do it. He showed forbearance. His love reached such a height that no human intellect could ever imagine. God came to earth! The second person of the Holy Trinity came to earth: our Lord Jesus Christ. He arrived in human flesh. He became a man like us, except for sin. He lived among us like the poorest of people. He served man with a love that the world experienced for the first time. He humbled Himself as no one else ever did. He became a servant of His servants. In the end He was crucified and shed his precious blood to save man. Every word, every miracle, every beat of His heart, every action, every drop of His blood shouts—everything shouts, everything preaches, everything declares: "God is love." His love is like an ocean.

After God has shown us so much love and continues to show us love, what should we feel toward Him, our benefactor? Shouldn't we feel the deepest kind of love and gratitude toward Him? Shouldn't we be willing to die rather than violate one of His commandments and sadden Him?

Unfortunately, we show the greatest ingratitude. Do you know what we are like? We are like a person to whom someone has extended hospitality, treated with kindness, and loved as no one else loved. When this person becomes sick and is in danger of dying, he is even given a transfusion with his friend's own blood and thus saved. And that person who has benefitted so much, instead of thanking his benefactor, turns and curses and blasphemes him, and spits in his face on leaving. I ask you: Is there such a person as that ungrateful and monstrous human being? There is! We are him, those of us who live in the twentieth century and sin. Under the cross of Christ's love, we continue the curses, the blasphemies, the mockings, and the spittings of those who crucified Him. Oh, what ingratitude, what horror! To such love, such aversion and evil! O Christ, forgive us!

## WHERE DO YOU WORK?

*For as ye have yielded your member servants to uncleanness and to iniquity unto iniquity; even so now yield your members to righteousness unto holiness.*

—Rom. 6:19

An edifice, my beloved, doesn't spring up by itself. The materials with which it is constructed do not appear by themselves either. Someone has to collect the steel, cement, bricks, iron, wood, and everything else that's needed. Once these materials become a heap at the site, the workers have to separate them, assemble them properly, and build them into an edifice, not in a hit-or-miss fashion but according to the plans that an architect has prepared beforehand. If the design is striking, the building will be admired by the people once it is finished. While marveling at and admiring beautiful buildings, people never think of them as being erected all by themselves. Rather, they willingly give credit to the craftsmen and technicians who put their efforts into creating these magnificent structures.

Do you marvel at such buildings? Today's homily comes to show you another building—a building that according to the plan, the materials, its harmony and grace, is incomparable. All of the architects, engineers, and technicians of the world cannot build this edifice, not even one of the smallest parts of it.

And just where might we visit this masterpiece of architecture, which is so praiseworthy? There is no need, beloved, to travel to view this wonderful edifice.

This edifice we are talking about is very near us. It is our body. Yes, our body. Have you ever found the time to sit down and examine every detail of the human body? Everything that the human body has is marvelous. It has different organs, each of which is a small factory destined to perform certain functions. All of the organs cooperate and help each other so that a person can live, move, and work. The heart, for example is a small pump that collects and circulates blood. The veins are the pipes that transfer the blood to all parts of the body. The nerves are the wires that transfer the orders of the brain. The kidneys are the filters that clean the fluids. The lungs are the ventilators. The stomach is a mill that grinds food. The eyes are a camera. The ears are radar. The hands are the proper instruments for all work. And the brain? Oh, the brain! It is a small handful of matter, weighing no more than two to three pounds. Yet inside this small amount of matter are various centers that receive information and impressions from everywhere.

Each one of the body's marvelous organs consists of very tiny components that are called cells. These cells are like small stones, like the bricks that a mason puts together. The human body consists of millions of them. The entire structure is so well balanced that it is based on only two columns, the legs, and it moves upright.

Aren't all of these things marvelous, beloved? What is the most perfect machine or the most perfect structure compared to the human body? And the question arises: What architect designed this edifice, the human body? Who took the various materials from which the body is composed and connected them in such a way that they are in the right place to execute certain functions? To all these questions there is only one logical answer: God. He fashioned man's body. He created the immortal soul that dwells in every person and is the moving force of thought and action. Without the soul, the body is dead.

Man's body is God's excellent creation. Unfortunately, there were heretics who accused it of being the spiritual enemy of man. Look at what it does, they said. The hands steal, grab, and hit; they are soaked in blood. The eyes look at the worst pictures. The ears hear awful things. The tongue drips poison—a worse poison than a viper's. The body, they said, is the cause of man's sins. The angels, who don't have bodies, don't sin, they said. And if people didn't have bodies, they wouldn't sin.

Is this idea of the heretics correct? Shall we blame and condemn the body as the source of the evils that plague human life?

The answer is in today's apostolic reading. According to the words of the Apostle Paul that we heard today, the body of a person and its various parts are the executing organs of the soul. We will explain this: A knife, for example, doesn't do anything by itself. If, however, people take it in their hands, it will do different jobs according to the wishes of those who hold it. If the baker holds it, it will cut bread; if the butcher takes it, it will cut meats; if the doctor takes it, it will become a scalpel; if the priest takes it, it will cut the bread for Holy Communion. If, however, an insane or evil man takes the knife, it will harm, kill, and spread disaster. Upon seeing those who were killed or injured by the knife of an insane man or criminal, can we say that the knife is at fault? Certainly not. Then, just as the knife becomes an instrument of good or evil according to the wishes of the person who holds it, in the same way the body becomes an instrument of good or evil, according to the desires of the soul that governs it. The soul, with thought, feelings, and its will, is the master that governs. The body is the servant, and the servant awaits the orders of its master. Everything depends on the soul. Is it corrupt? Does it have evils, vices, and passions that govern it? If so, it will order the body to do whatever it wishes. Is the soul, for example, possessed by hatred and animosity? Does it despise someone? Does it want to kill someone? Then it will order the hand to take the weapon and commit the murder? Or maybe the soul is possessed by anger and wrath It will order the tongue to become a machine gun that shoots another person.

The body isn't just the servant of evil. It can become the servant of good, too. Is the soul charitable? The hand will become like the hand of the farmer who takes seed and scatters it in a field. In the same way, the hand of a charitable person spreads good to those who are in need. Or is the soul faithful and pious, with a deep feeling of love and gratitude for God? The tongue will become an instrument that sings of His blessings and grandeur.

Oh soul, for whom do you work? For the devil or for God? If you work for the devil, then all of the parts of your body will become tools that will do evil and spread misfortune. If, however, you work for God, your body will be sanctified, and all of its parts will become instruments that will always do good and spread joy and happiness. Soul, for whom do you work? Again I ask you, for God or for the devil? Choose God as your master, and then, beloved, you will be truly happy and blessed.

# DEPOSITION OF THE ROBE OF THE THEOTOKOS
Hebrews 9:1–7

## WITHOUT CHURCHES?

*The priests went always into the first tabernacle,*
*accomplishing the service of God. But into the second*
*went the high priest alone once every year.*
—Heb. 9:6-7

My beloved Christians, there isn't a people on earth who haven't got a religion. Even in those countries that claim to be atheistic and persecute the faith, yes, even in those countries, there are people who believe in God and express their religious feelings by worshiping Him in places where the police can't find them.

All people of the world are religious to one degree or another—some more so, some less so. Among these people, there was a group who was religious in an absolute sense: the Hebrews. They had the privilege of believing in the true God. They had organized their personal, domestic, communal, and national life according to His commandments. The Hebrew nation was a theocratic one. God reigned among the people, and they worshiped Him, offering sacrifices not only on Saturday, but every day. Where did they worship Him? When they were slaves of the Egyptians, their tyrants didn't allow them to build their own temple, so they worshiped God in their homes and in their hearts. When God, through Moses, freed them, the Hebrews started out for their beloved homeland. Then they worshiped God openly. Where? Being obliged to walk every day, they couldn't build a temple. So God directed them to build a movable one that they could dismantle and put up anywhere. And so they fashioned one using boards, skins of animals, and fine materials. They called it the Tabernacle.

What a tabernacle! The Hebrew people lived in tents while they wandered in the desert. These were their homes. Among these tents, these movable habitations of theirs, was a tent that was different from all the rest. It was the Tabernacle, the movable temple. Those of you who have been in the army and served your country during those awful days of war will remember with great feeling how the chaplain improvised an altar and celebrated Divine Liturgy high up in the mountains where there weren't any churches. The Hebrews did the same thing during the years they were wandering in the desert. They had the Tabernacle, and inside it they kept the holiest things of their religion. The tabernacle was divided into two parts by large, thick curtains, or veils. One side of the Tabernacle was called the Holies. The second side was called the Holy of Holies. The high priest entered this section once a year and offered a sacrifice, asking forgiveness for his sins and for the sins of the people.

The Hebrews worshiped the true God in that Tabernacle. When, however, they were settled in their homeland and after many adventures and struggles succeeded in becoming the most powerful kingdom of the East, they felt urge to build a temple in Jerusalem, the capital of their kingdom. They wanted the temple to be the largest building in the kingdom—a great example of Hebrew glory and power, and an ethnic and religious center. One of the most glorious kings of Israel, Solomon, the son of David, built it. That is why it was called Solomon's temple. The whole world marveled at it. It was built with carved stones, multicolored marble, and rare woods; its walls and roof were covered with gold. Its design didn't differ significantly from the plan of the Tabernacle, for just as the Tabernacle was divided into two parts, the temple itself was divided into two parts. The dedication took place with great solemnity, and the joy of the people was unimaginable.

The Hebrew people worshiped inside this temple of Solomon for four hundred years. But when they sinned, a great calamity occurred. An impious king, Nebuchadnezzar, came out of Babylon with an army like a torrent. He defeated the Jews, conquered Jerusalem, tore down the temple of Solomon, and took thousands of prisoners back to Babylon. After many years the captive people returned to Jerusalem. They started to build houses, but they didn't have a temple. "Shame on you," the prophet Haggai then said, "you build beautiful homes but you don't have a temple." Thus they were moved to build a temple. The leader of this effort was Zorobabel. After countless difficulties and obstacles, they built the temple. It was a splendid temple but inferior to the first one. The older people who had seen the temple of Solomon as children compared the one with the other, saw the great difference, and wept.

The Hebrews worshiped God in this new temple for five hundred years. But again disaster struck. Enemies conquered Israel and destroyed this temple, too. On its ruins Herod the Great built a new one, which was decorated with marble and gold. It was also a very beautiful temple. The All Holy Virgin Mary brought Christ to it when He was twelve years old. He stood in its forecourt many times and preached. And He prophesied that this temple, too, would be destroyed and that not a stone would remain on top of another stone. Christ's prophecy was fulfilled thirty years after His crucifixion when the Romans came and conquered Jerusalem. They set fire to the city, tore down the temple, and killed and crucified thousands. Despite 1,900 years having passed since that time, the Hebrews haven't managed to build another temple. Every Saturday pious Hebrews go and cry at the cornerstones that remain from that temple.

What does all this teach us? First of all, that building and having a temple will please God; He commands it. He spoke, and the first Tabernacle was made—the Tabernacle of the Witness. Then He blessed the building of the temple of Solomon. When Christ Himself came into the world, He went to the temple and worshiped and prayed like a man. All Christian people have their churches and temples. Only Jehovah's Witnesses don't have any, don't want to step inside them, and don't want to bless themselves.

The second thing that we are taught is that it isn't enough to build and have temples. Something else, something more important and indispensable, is needed. When we hear the bell ringing, our hearts must be moved. We must say: God is calling me. We must go to church with desire. We must stand with reverence. We must listen to the Divine Liturgy attentively and pray with tears and contrition. Receive the immaculate sacraments with fear, faith, and love, and live according to the will of God. If we do this, then we are worshiping God in the way the Bible wants us to: "In spirit and in truth." And His blessings will be with us. What if we don't? What if we fill up the shopping malls, amusement parks, and football stadiums on Sundays and leave the churches empty? What if we go to church but our minds are not on God? What if we gossip and sin in and outside of church and live like heathens and Antichrists? Oh, then woe be unto us! God's wrath will come upon us. Our houses and churches will be torn down, and we will be punished for our unbelief and impiety.

# THE SIXTH SUNDAY OF MATTHEW
Romans 12:6–14

## GIFTS

*Having then gifts differing according to the grace that is given to us.*

—Rom. 12:6

The Apostolic reading that we heard today, beloved, speaks about gifts. We, too, shall speak about gifts, and I ask you to please pay attention.

First of all, what are gifts? Gifts are the abilities people have. Because these abilities are different, the gifts are also different. There are physical gifts, mental gifts, and spiritual gifts. Let us mention a few examples so that we can better understand what they are.

Let us consider physical gifts. A person is tall, has beautiful bearing, and has a good-looking face. We might be describing a man, but more likely a woman, who draws attention and admiration. Her beauty is a gift. Another person isn't good looking but is strong. He can pick up weights that three other people together can't lift. He can do heavy work from morning till night and not tire. Bodily strength is a gift, just as much as the ability to run fast is a gift. The runner's gift is being able to run a distance that someone else can run in two hours in half an hour. Another person has the gift of great health. Only those who have been seriously ill and spent days in agony can appreciate what a valuable gift good health is.

Now let's look at mental gifts. A student hears what the teacher says and stores the information in his brain. That student has the gift of memory. Another student solves a problem in mathematics with great ease. She has the gift of mathematics. Another person takes a brush and paints a beautiful portrait of Christ. He has the gift of painting. Another gets enthused by all that she sees in the physical world and writes beautiful poems. She has the gift of poetry. Another takes the violin and makes the strings come alive, producing music that moves the audience to tears. He has the gift of music. And so on.

The talents and abilities that we have mentioned in relation to life, art, and science are gifts because they come from God. That people don't have the same abilities but different ones is also a mystery that serves God's plan. A father who has many children sees this. Even though all of his children live under the same roof and have the same upbringing, each of them has his or her own inclinations and his or her own gifts. One wants to become a farmer and live a quiet life. The second wants to become a shepherd, climb the mountains, play the flute, and praise the magnificence of nature, glorifying God. The third is charmed by the sea and wants to become a sea captain. The fourth is inclined toward mechanics. They all have different inclinations and different drives.

People have different gifts. We said that this is a mystery that serves God's plan. If everyone had the same abilities and the same gifts, a community wouldn't be able to survive. Imagine a community where everyone is a doctor or lawyer or mechanic or teacher. It would be impossible for that community to function. Perhaps with only farmers and shepherds it could, but then again the community wouldn't be complete. So we see the hand of God providing this variety of physical and mental gifts. He distributes to people whatever they need with wisdom and love, not simply so that they can live but to create a bond—a society in which everyone feels the need for everyone else.

We have to marvel even more at the wisdom of God when we look at the Church. Christ established this new community, the Church, so that man could live a better life. Inside the church there are spiritual gifts. And what are they? One Christian has the gift of compassion. When he hears that something unfortunate has happened to a neighboring family, he visits the family and with compassionate words from his heart consoles and encourages them. Upon his consoling words, the family who was in despair and ready to give up takes courage and starts to live again with new hope. To be someone who can console others is a gift. Giving alms to those who don't have anything and are suffering is a gift—the gift of charity. Opening the Bible to read the words of Christ is also a gift—the gift of Holy Scripture. Kneeling to pray is a gift—the gift of prayer. Going to church to celebrate the liturgy is also a gift—the gift of psalmody. An even greater gift is to become a priest, to celebrate the holy mysteries, to preach the word of God, and to sanctify people. In addition to these gifts, there are some extraordinary gifts in the Church. A special one is for a Christian to be able to expel demons from the possessed with prayer. Another special gift is to be able to prophecy events one hundred or two hundred years from now. St. Cosmas Aetolos, who prophesied many of the things that are taking place today, had that kind of gift.

The gifts that we see in the Church are spiritual gifts, because the Holy Spirit gives them. He doesn't give them to unbelieving and wicked people but to people who believe and live according to His will. He gives them, as today's Apostolic reading says, "according to the grace." What does this mean? It means that someone who goes to the river gets as much water as the container that he takes with him will hold. If he has a pitcher, he will get as much water as the pitcher holds. If he has a jug, he will get more. If he has a barrel, even more. The quantity of water depends on the size of the container he takes with him. We are speaking parabolically. The river is God's grace, a spiritual river. So run, my Christian, and get water from it. A proper container with which to get this water is faith. Do you have little faith? You will get a small gift. Do you have great faith? You will get a great gift. If we had the faith that the saints and martyrs of our Church had, we would see the power of God moving, and miraculous things would happen through us.

God, my beloved, is the One Who gives us these different gifts. These gifts, as we've seen, are physical, mental, and spiritual. He doesn't give them to us so that we can hide them, but to use them and multiply them for the benefit of society, for the progress of the Church, and for the glory of God. Whatever we have belongs to God. Only our sins belong to us. Our gifts are God's, and we have a great responsibility because of them. We will have to give a strict accounting as to how we have used them, for we are the administrators of someone else's money here. We will have to account for what we have done with it to the very last penny. And may God have mercy on us!

# THE LANGUAGE OF THE HERETICS

*But avoid foolish questions, and genealogies, and
contentions, and strivings about the law; for they are
unprofitable and vain.*

—Titus 3:9

Language, my beloved Christians, is a special privilege
people have. By language, we mean the ability that a
person has to express his or her thoughts and feelings.
Animals also have tongues. The monkey, from whom
some foolish people say man descends, has a tongue. But
though the monkey and the other animals have tongues,
they cannot speak because they don't have thoughts or
ideas. Man, however, speaks because he has a mind that
thinks, and his tongue is the instrument which expresses
his internal world. Without this organ, man would have
a problem communicating what he thinks and what he
wants. We see this in the case of deaf-mutes, who
communicate with different movements of their hands.

Language, for man, is an instrument of the soul
for good or for evil. With language, man can do thousands
of good things. With language, a mother teaches her child
its first words. She teaches her child to say a little prayer
before the statue of Christ. With language, the grand-
mother tells her grandchildren beautiful stories that they
won't forget. With language, the teacher imparts knowledge that is necessary for learning. With language, the
university professor explains scientific principles. With
language, the doctor communicates with the sick person,
offering consolation and encouragement. With language,
the lawyer defends an innocent client in court. With

language, the district attorney prosecutes the criminal and asks for an appropriate punishment. With language, the brave officer urges the soldiers under his command to fight the sacred fight for the faith and for country. With language, the priest blesses the faithful, invokes the All Holy Spirit, and celebrates the mysteries. With language, the preacher urges the people to repent and return to God. And so on.

Oh, how many good things happen with language! But many evil things can happen in this world with language. Man babbles with language. With language, man speaks with a filthy tongue. With language, man slanders and insults people, inciting hatred and animosity. With language, man offends the honor of the family of another, maligning innocent people and pouring poison into their hearts and lives. With language, man tells thousands of lies; rarely does man speak the truth. With language, the immoral person urges young boys and girls to explore illicit sex. With language, the heretic spreads the infection of error and heresy. With language, the atheist teaches unbelief in God. With language, man blasphemes Christ, the king of all.

Oh, how many evils language commits in this world. How many crimes and killings it causes. For a word is like a match that you light and toss into a forest, and causing a fire that burns it all. With one match! In the same way, one word can bring about great evil.

The Apostle Paul knows what horrors the language of evil and corrupt people—unbelievers, atheists, and heretics—can bring. Paul himself experienced this evil, because wherever he went and preached to people with his heavenly tongue, Satan tried to destroy what he did through the tongues of heretical and unbelieving people. Unfortunately, many people paid more attention to what these organs of Satan said than to the words of the Apostle. What a strange thing, to listen to heretics and not to Paul! The heretics' words were false; they told stories like the stories the ancient idolaters told about their false gods. And just as there was an idolatrous mythology, in the same way there was a Judaic mythology, which the heretics of the time created through their fantasies. These heretics made the small and unimportant seem great and important; at the same time, the important and great they made small and unimportant. They did something even worse: They called darkness light and the light, darkness. They hated the light, and they hated Christ; they did everything to extinguish the light and to dissolve the Church.

When the heretics went to Crete, Paul wrote to his disciple Titus, the first bishop of Crete, warning him to be careful and not to waste time meeting with the heretics. He told Titus that even if he were to meet them one or two times, they wouldn't change their minds. He warned Titus that they were perverse people, and no matter what he said to them, they would not change.

Today, there are similar heretics, the millenniasts who call themselves Jehovah's Witnesses. They have spread to cities and villages everywhere. Their language is similar to the language of the ancient heretics. Like the heretics, they tell many stories. Their big story is that all nations will be destroyed one day, and only one nation, the Hebrew Empire, will dominate the world. Its capital will be Jerusalem. Its prime minister will be Abraham. Its ministers, the prophets and patriarchs. All of these people, they say, will be resurrected and will govern the world for a thousand years. And for a thousand years, people will live happily in a Hebrew paradise, which will be full of all of the good things of the world.

Around this story Jehovah's Witnesses fabricate other stories, trying to base them on passages of Scripture which they misinterpret and distort. Their followers go from factory to factory, from office to office, and from house to house. Wherever they find some naive person, they start preaching their satanic lies. The language of the millenniasts, you would say, drips with honey. It is sweet, but poison is hidden in it—the poison of error and impiety. Whoever listens to them and is unable to separate truth from fiction is caught in their nets, and it is very difficult to get out of them.

The question arises: What stand should Orthodox Christians take against these heretics, these unbelievers and atheists? They shouldn't start any discussions with them, as the Apostle counsels us today. They should throw them out of their houses. They should inform the diocese that a wolf has appeared in the fold, so that the bishop can take the spiritual measures that are required to protect his flock. He will send a theologian to the village. The theologian will invite the Jehovah's Witnesses to an open, public discussion to prove that what they say is a lie, deceit, and distortion. The language of Orthodoxy will defeat the language of the heretics. But you, Oh Christian, who cannot recognize the cunning of these people, get away from them. Get away from them just as you would get away from a poisonous snake. It would be better to be bitten by a snake than to be bitten by the language of the millenniasts.

# THE EIGHTH SUNDAY OF MATTHEW
1 Corinthians 1:10–17

## WHO WAS CRUCIFIED?

*Is Christ divided? Was Paul crucified for you?*
—1 Cor. 1:13

Apostle Paul, my beloved, writes to the Christians of Corinth in today's Epistle. At that time, Corinth was one of the largest cities in the world. Because it was built near the sea, on the famous isthmus of Corinth, it had developed into an important naval and commercial center of the Mediterranean. Thousands of ships passed through its harbor. Its people lived in luxury and self-indulgence. Large numbers of immoral women lived at the notorious temple of Venus, which the pagan Greeks had built to honor that shameful deity.

Philosophers and orators came from the neighboring city of Athens and were paid to teach the youth in Corinth deceit and lying. For this reason, much filth collected in the city: prostitution, adultery, self-indulgence, avarice, envy, and every other evil littered the streets. Satan knew that he had to cover such filth with a thin layer of gold, with the pseudophilosophies of the ancients, so that the ugliness wouldn't be seen.

Christ wasn't known in Corinth when the preachers of the Bible came to the city. The Apostle Paul stayed for a year and a half, preaching with a fiery heart and calling the people to believe in the Crucified One. His preaching brought about very good results. People who had been steeped in depravity, came out of the mire. They believed, were baptized, and became Christians. It was one of the most moving sights that the power of Christianity presented. Because of the preaching of the Apostle Paul, as well as other apostles and preachers of the Bible, the first church was established in Corinth. But the Christians didn't have any place to worship because the idolaters did not allow them to build churches; nor were Christians allowed to congregate publicly. So those who believed in Christ would gather secretly in certain Christian homes to pray and celebrate the mystery of the Holy Eucharist. All these people were united in the name of Christ. They became a large family whose members were connected by their faith and love for Christ.

That the Church of Corinth was united was a joy to Paul and a sorrow to the demons, because Satan hates nothing more than seeing Christians who are united and loving. Satan tried to divide the Church, and for a little while he succeeded. Most of the Christians were Greeks, and unfortunately they have an awful hereditary vice, discord—that is, Greeks find it difficult to get along with each other. Even if they agree on something, it doesn't last very long. Every one of them is proud and egotistical; he raises his own flag and revolts against spiritual leadership. Thus religious factions sprouted up in Corinth, and the few Christians were divided. Some made Paul their leader; others chose Apollo, who was a dynamic orator; still others followed Peter, who was the best-known Apostle and disciple of the Lord, their leader.

"No!" shouts Paul to the Corinthians. "What you are doing is wrong. Neither I nor Peter nor Apollo came to your city asking for honors and glories. What are we? We are nothing. Whatever you have you have from Christ. Christ is everything. Christ created the world from nothing. Christ created man. Christ gives mankind whatever it needs to live. The water, the light, the air are His. Everything is His. And if He stops concerning Himself about man for a few moments, how can man live?"

Paul puts aside these material blessings and reminds the Corinthians of the greatest of all of the benevolent acts that Christ performed—a benevolence that will be declared to all of the ages: that no one else loved mankind as much as He did. This blessing, for which there is no measure to measure it with, or scale to weigh, is that Christ was crucified and shed His precious blood for mankind.

Yes, the cross is the greatest proof of divine love. Without the sacrifice that Christ offered on it, no one could be saved. But, certainly, most Christians don't feel this way. They are not moved when they hear that Christ was crucified for them. The small acts of charity that other people do for them, move them. If, for example, someone is in danger of dying and needs blood, the sick person feels a deep gratitude for the person who donated the blood. And if the person gets well, he or she might send a warm letter to the newspaper thanking the donor. But what Christ did, by opening His veins and transfusing His blood into a humanity that was sick and dying from sins, unfortunately, does not move many people. His blood doesn't sing in their hearts. The cross doesn't stir them. They're indifferent.

Without the cross, without the blood that the God-man shed on that awful hill of Golgotha, the Church wouldn't exist. It exists because Christ was sacrificed. It exists because every time the bell rings and Christians gather, that sacrifice is repeated, and His precious blood is offered to them in a mysterious way "for the remission of sins and life eternal."

Wishing to strike at the divisions between the Christians and to unite them, Paul mentions the cross as the strongest argument. Who was crucified? he asks. Who shed his blood? Whose blood was able to wash away the sins of the whole world? If a thousand Pauls, a thousand Apollos, and a thousand Peters were to shed their blood, it wouldn't wipe away even one sin, because all of them, without exception, are sinners and need forgiveness and redemption.

Only one person can save us; only one person can redeem us: Christ. All of us who preach Him, we are nothing before Him. We are His slaves; we are His servants. Why, then, are we haughty? Why do we boast? Why do we divide the Church and put ourselves forth and want to raise the "I" inside the Church of Christ?

Oh these "I's!" They fractionalize the Church. And these "I's" have to be eliminated. Only when the little and the great "I's" are submitted to the will of the One, to Him Who with His precious blood established the Church, only then will all of the schisms and all of the divisions vanish. then a united Church will appear as bright as the sun, without clouds and without shadows.

# THE NINTH SUNDAY OF MATTHEW
1 Corinthians 3:9–17

## ONE BUILDING

*For we are labourers together with God: ye are God's husbandry, ye are God's building.*

—1 Cor. 3:9

Not long ago, beloved, the following happened in Thessalonica. In a certain part of the city an apartment building was built. All of the work had been finished. From the outside, it appeared very beautiful. Inside, the apartments were tastefully decorated. They were soon rented. Everything in the building seemed pleasant, until one day when disaster struck. The building began to shake, and all those who were inside listening to their radios and televisions were frightened and thought the end of the world had come. They ran out as quickly as they could. What happened? An earthquake? No. The engineer who had built the apartment building hadn't paid enough attention to the foundation. He had set it in a place where the ground was soft, and the building had settled. The building was left with only the furniture, radios, and television sets in it, empty of people. Eventually, it was declared unsafe, and a construction company demolished it.

Thus an apartment building in Thessalonica was torn down. But it isn't the only one. Other buildings collapse and kill the people who are not able to get out in time. Unfortunately, in their effort to make more money, dishonest engineers and contractors skimp on the foundations. Of course, the foundations are underground and hidden from view. The builders concentrate on the parts of the building that can be seen and will impress those who are looking for a place to rent. But what's the use if everything seems in order and is beautiful but the foundation isn't solid? Buildings without solid foundations fall down sooner or later and become ruins.

Why are we speaking about buildings and foundations? Of what interest are they to us, you will ask. We aren't engineers or contractors; neither do we have the money to buy condominiums and apartment buildings. We are poor people. We live in our little houses, the same ones our parents and grandparents lived in. Two hundred years have passed since they were built, and nothing has happened to them. We love our ancestral homes, and wouldn't exchange them for all the apartment buildings and skyscrapers in New York. Solid houses, my friend; solid houses are what everyone should look for if they want to live securely.

Besides these material dwellings, there is another kind of dwelling, a spiritual one, whose one part is visible and the other, invisible. It is the edifice that starts on earth and reaches the stars. It is an edifice that surpasses in structure, beauty, and solidity every other building. The Apostle Paul speaks about this building, this spiritual edifice, today.

What is this spiritual building? It is the Church. But when we say Church, what do we mean? Do we mean the temple of our parish, the building that we've built so we can gather and worship God? Certainly, that building is called a church, but *the* Church is primarily all those who believe in Christ, partake of the immaculate mysteries, are joined among themselves with His love, and consider each other as brothers and sisters. These are the people who compose the Church, the spiritual edifice, about which Paul speaks. And thus Paul calls it the Church because there are certain similarities between a physical and a spiritual edifice. Look at some of them.

To be solid a building must have a firm foundation. It must be built upon a rock. In the same way, the Church, the spiritual edifice, also has a foundation. Its solid and unshakable foundation is our Lord Jesus Christ. Its foundation is faith in Christ—the faith that Christ isn't simply a man, like all other men, but is God, the true God Who descended from heaven to earth, appeared in human form, hungered, thirsted, preached, was crucified, arose and ascended to heaven, and shall come again to judge the world. Christ is the Alpha and the Omega. Christ is everything.

On this faith is built the spiritual edifice, the Church. Christ Himself said it to Peter, when Peter professed that Christ is the true God. "You," He said to Peter, "must be called Peter because of this faith, and I assure you that on this faith I shall build the Church, and it shall be so firm and unshakable that all of the evil forces that come out of their dark Kingdom to fight against it will not be able to defeat it." This is the interpretation of Christ's words: "Thou art Peter, and upon this rock I will build my church, and the gates of hell shall not prevail against it." (Matt. 16:18)

Just as the rocks on a foundation, some smaller, some bigger, are set in the earth and connected with concrete so that they become one unit, so, too, is the Church. Those who believe in Christ aren't far from each other spiritually, but like the stones of a foundation, they compose one body, one community. The cement that connects them in this divine edifice is love. Without love, the unity of Christians resembles a wall that is built without cement and can easily fall. The builders, who must select the stones, that is to say find Christians who are willing to give up their vices and evils, are the priests. Just as in a building there is a crane that raises the stones to be placed in their proper places, in the same way, we might say, the machine that takes the Christians from below and raises them up is the cross of Christ. Yes! The cross, a certain saint says, like a machine, takes believers and raises them to the heights. This spiritual edifice could not gain height without the power of the cross.

My beloved! An edifice that rises from a foundation has a peak, too. But the spiritual edifice, the Church, has been built now continuously for twenty centuries. New Christians, like living stones, are added, and the edifice continuously progresses; no one will be able to stop its progress. It will grow until the end of the ages, until the last believer is added.

To this edifice, the Orthodox Church, we, too, belong, my beloved readers. Great Fathers, saints, and martyrs were its pillars and columns. But what are we? We will be happy if we become a little stone in the vast and magnificent structure that is called the Orthodox Church.

# THE TRANSFIGURATION OF THE SAVIOUR
2 Peter 1:10–19

## A REMINDER

*Yea, I think it meet, as long as I am in this tabernacle,
to stir you up by putting you in remembrance.*

—2 Pet. 1:13

 Someone, my beloved, who owes money doesn't forget his debt. He remembers it and tries to pay it back. But if he forgets and it comes due, the bank sends him a piece of paper called a reminder. That is to say, the bank reminds him of the debt he has forgotten and asks him to pay it back. If he doesn't pay it back in due time, there will be certain consequences.

Besides the debts that people owe to other people, to banks, and to lending institutions, there are other debts—debts that all people in general have. The curious thing is, that as one's wealth increases, so do one's debts. The debts we are now talking about are the responsibilities and duties that we owe to ourselves, our neighbors, and God. Salvation of our souls is a duty—that is, to believe, to weep, and to repent for all the sins we have committed. Self-improvement is a duty—that is, to cleanse ourselves of our evils and vices and to grow in virtue. The salvation of our neighbor is a duty—that is, to offer to help our fellow man meet different material and spiritual needs. To cry with the afflicted is a duty, as well as to feel joy for their joys. To spread the Gospel to all the world is a duty, as well as to forgive even our enemies. Toward God our duty is to thank Him day and night from the bottom of our hearts for all the blessings He gives us, and to glorify Him for all the great and miraculous things that we see in the natural and spiritual world. It is our duty to ask God to forgive us for our sins and to give us His grace to do His will with eagerness and zeal.

Oh, man is full of duties and responsibilities! And as we have said, as we get richer, mightier, and more glorious, our duties increase. The poor, the illiterate, and the unimportant have few responsibilities, but those who have millions, who have climbed to great offices, have great responsibilities.

Some people do remember their duties and responsibilities. But unfortunately, most people forget them and live indifferently. They neglect themselves; they let their neighbor die of hunger and misfortune; they forget God.

What must be done with these people? Should they stay like this? Should they live indifferently and senselessly? No, of course not. Others must remind them of their duties.

The Apostle Peter emphasizes the spiritual duty people have for other people in today's Epistle on the feast of the Transfiguration. Who was Peter? He was an Apostle of Christ who had received the commandment from Him to preach the Gospel to the whole world. Peter never stopped performing this commandment. He continuously taught, admonished, and reproved the world. "I will not stop reminding you," he writes to the Christians, "of your obligations." Peter knew how easily a person forgets the good that he hears, but evil, if heard just once, imprints itself vividly in the mind, where it won't unglue itself. Evil heard when a person is a child will be remembered in old age. Whatever good a person hears is soon forgotten. That is why the father, mother, teacher, priest, or preacher must frequently remind the child about the good teaching.

"I will not stop," says Peter to the Christians, "to remind you about what I have taught you. Not simply to remind you, but rouse you—that is, to speak to you with vigor, to wake you up and urge you to the good." Socrates, an ancient philosopher of our country, said something similar. "I am," he said to the ancient Athenians, "like an ox goad." What is an ox goad? The farmer pricks the oxen that sit lazily in the barn with it and makes them come out, get into the yoke, and plow. When the farmer plows, the goad is never missing from his hand. If it is, the oxen will stop. Goading, you see, is necessary. "What the farmer does to the oxen I do to you," says Socrates. "The goad is my words. And no matter how severe and bitter they might seem, they become the reason everyone sees his ignorance, his evil and corruption, and tries to correct himself. You, certainly, are irritated by my criticism, and you want me to stop teaching and criticizing you. You want me to break the goad. You are ready to condemn me to death. But if you kill me, then there will be no one to wake you and remind you of your duties. Without the goad, you will live indifferently, and you will sleep like animals in the barn. You will sleep until the good God has pity on you and sends someone else who will come to wake you."

So continuous teaching, continuous reminding is necessary. But is it happening? Unfortunately, no. Those who are obligated to teach, to instruct, and to criticize the people neglect their duties. When Peter and Paul were in prison, they didn't stop sending letters, reminding the Christians in a lively way to remember their preaching. But what are we, today's teachers and successors in their work, doing? Are we continuously reminding our fellow Christians of their duties? Most of us think that by giving a sermon—and a lukewarm one at that—once a week or even less frequently, we are performing our duties. Alas, how we fall short, how far we are from it! In our time, which is like the time of Sodom and Gomorrah, we need many ox goads. We need reproving and lively sermons. We need continuous reminders—reminders written with pain, tears, and even blood like the blood that the martyrs shed to awaken the consciences of sinners and of the guilty.

Saint Peter! You, who at the top of Mt. Tabor was made worthy enough to see the glory of Christ, we beg you, entreat the Lord to give strength to those who preach the Gospel, so that they may not tire, but continuously and in a lively way remind the people about their spiritual duties and preach the truth of the Gospel until death.

# THE ELEVENTH SUNDAY OF MATTHEW
1 Corinthians 9:2–12

# THE DEFENDANT!

*Mine answer to them that do examine me is this.*
—1 Cor. 9:3

Beloved, have you seen a court in session? On the bench is the judge. At the stand is the defendant, accused of some crime. The witnesses against the defendant testify to many things that make his position worse. Witnesses in his behalf do not appear. He is alone! The prosecutor is severe. He outlines the crime, explains why he believes the defendant is guilty, and demands a severe judgment against him. The defendant is silent and frightened.

Someone is sitting on the defendant's stand, as we see in today's apostolic reading. He isn't sitting there for the first time. His vicious enemies have brought him before the courts of district governors and generals many other times. The defendant apologizes and succeeds in convincing them that he is innocent and is freed from his chains. But who is the defendant? And who are his accusers? The defendant is Paul. Paul? But what did he do wrong? What crime did he commit for which he is accused? Is it theft? Prostitution? Adultery? Murder? Unbelief and atheism? None of these. The defendant didn't commit these kinds of crimes. Paul was a man who always did good. He was a exceptional man. A rare man. What am I saying? No one else like him was born or ever will be born. Of all the Christians, through all the centuries, Paul was the one who imitated Christ the most.

Paul was the apostle of the nations, the greatest. So who would expect him to be accused of any crime? Yet there were people who brought charges against him.

His enemies were not just unbelievers and atheists, and idol-worshiping kings and governors who, understandably, hated and persecuted him and used every means to destroy him; his enemies also were people who knew him closely, who heard his warm and life-giving teaching, and who saw his holy life and the miracles he performed. And yet these evil people, these pseudo-Christians, brought charges against him. They accused him, among other charges, of committing slander. But if there was a charge that hurt Paul more than any other, it was the accusation that he wasn't a true Apostle. Those who hated him compared him with the other preachers of the Bible and found, supposedly, that he was inferior. They said he didn't have the gifts the others had. Nor did he have a pleasing appearance. He was not eloquent and had no philosophy. They said his words were meaningless. Only when he wrote, did they give him a little credit. "We don't want to hear him," they said. "We listen only to the other apostles and preachers of the Bible, the ones who are important." Paul? With such contempt did his enemies refer to him!

Paul's enemies, through their malicious words and gossip, tried to undermine the confidence the Christians had placed in him. They also undermined Paul's preaching. Thus, those who had believed in Christ through Paul's preaching were in danger of losing their faith altogether and returning to their old religion, idolatry. From the light, that is to say, they would return to darkness—from truth to lies, from Christ to the Devil—what a catastrophe!

The danger was great. Paul could not remain indifferent. It wasn't simply a matter of personal honor and reputation, but something greater—a matter of faith. Paul answered his accusers. He described various incidents in his life and proved how pure his motives were. No mere concern, no self-interest possessed him. He did not take money from anyone. He did not eat free bread. He and his companions worked for a living. He put himself in danger every day. He had but one purpose: to guide sinners to Christ by spreading the light he saw to souls who lived in darkness. "I would not write," he said, "of the sacrifices I made for Christ, I wouldn't write about my accomplishments. But since my enemies accuse me and question everything, and want to say that neither I nor my preaching has any value, and you who hear the accusations, do not defend me, I am forced to defend myself and prove my innocence." This is the meaning of Paul's words when he wrote: "Mine answer to them that do examine me is this."

Paul a defendant! Who would have expected this? But why are we wondering? Christ Himself, Who is incomparably greater than Paul and all of the saints, was accused by the world, by His enemies. He was arrested, and as a defendant in bonds, stood before the unjust judges Annas, Caiaphas, and Pilate. So, let no one be surprised to see how a world that strayed far from God hates, accuses, and slanders the true workers of the Bible who struggle to bring the light and truth to today's generation. The world—the faithless world that is evil and corrupt and ready to applaud the most unimportant people—this same world is ready to insult, slander, and defame the preachers of Christ. This world continuously seats the faithful servants of Christ on the defendant's benches, and if it could, it would crucify them with sharper nails than those with which it crucified Christ and the Apostles.

My beloved! Allow me now, because the subject relates, to talk about myself—that is, to defend myself because I, too, am continuously accused by people who hate the light and the truth. For every action, for every word of ours, the unbelievers have something to say. Wherever, with the help of God, we try to light the holy fire, to burn away every evil and every sin, these people are standing by to throw snow to extinguish our efforts and spread despair on every good thing that happens in our diocese. The opposition seems to increase as more good is being done. Certainly, these people are few in number, but they do as much damage as they can. If they could, they would prevent us not only from preaching but also from living even a day longer.

In spite of all the opposition, however, we will continue our work as a bishop of the Orthodox Church. We will preach the word of God. We will support the doctrine of the Church. We will defend Orthodoxy. We will defend ourselves against our accusers. And to all those who want to see how we answer our accusers, I say, let them read a new book, *An Account of a Four-Year Period*. It is my defense as a bishop. On the very first page of this book, today's scriptural verse is written: "Mine answer to them that do examine me is this."

# THE TWELFTH SUNDAY OF MATTHEW
1 Corinthians 15:1-11

## GRACE

*But by the grace of God I am what I am.*
—1 Cor. 15:10

Paul! My beloved, Paul's enemies, as we talked about in last Sunday's homily, were trying to diminish his stature and present him as a small and unimportant man. History, however, recognizes Paul as one of the greatest spirits, and the Church sings his praises and calls him chief of the Apostles, Apostle of the nations. And rightly so, because no other apostle worked as hard as did Paul. In spite of the difficulties, the slander, the everyday dangers he faced, he did not bend. With a burning love, with steadfast faith, with patience and unbelievable persistence, with utmost humility and self-denial, with prudence and wisdom, and foremost with indomitable courage, Paul preached Christ and kindled the light in countless souls. Like an eagle with golden wings, Paul flew to the east and west, raising the flag of Christ on the strongest castles of the devil and in the greatest centers of idolatry. In the name of Christ, Paul expelled demons, cured the sick, raised the dead, and performed many other great miracles. His greatest miracles, which continue to help the world, were his fourteen Epistles. These Epistles are eternal miracles. In the end Paul sealed his holy life with his blood, becoming a martyr in Rome during Nero's reign.

Who among the preachers of the Bible through the centuries, I ask, can be compared to Paul? If Judas shows what corruption and depravity a man can reach, Paul, on the other hand, shows what great heights a person can reach. Paul lived in human flesh, but he lived like an angel, a heavenly man. That is why he was made worthy, while he still lived, to ascend to the third heaven beyond the sun and the stars, to ascend to paradise and the glory of God.

If someone else had accomplished only a small part of what Paul did, that person would be very proud. For example, here is a priest, who does almost nothing but because he wears a robe and people respect his priesthood, thinks there is no one else like him, and he talks about himself as an egotist. But Paul doesn't resemble us small and unimportant but proud people. Paul was very humble. "Whatever I have," Paul states, "is Christ's. Whatever I do I owe to His power." That is why Paul says: "But by the grace of God I am what I am."

To God's grace I owe everything, Paul confesses publicly. But what is this grace?

Certain things, beloved, we know exist but cannot see—for example, electricity. Who doubts that electricity exists? We see the results of its power. We see the light that it produces. We see the machines and the factories that it fuels. We see that enough electricity passes through a wire to electrocute a person. Although we see the results of electricity, we cannot see electricity itself. What is electricity? Not even the greatest scientists of the world can give us a satisfactory answer. They can describe its peculiarities and results, but they cannot give us its definition or explain its secret. Electricity is visible in relation to its results; however, in relation to its essence, it is invisible.

We bring up electricity as an example, to help explain the idea of grace, about which the Apostle Paul speaks today. Grace! Please pay attention, because the subject is very important for our salvation.

Divine grace is not a physical power, like electricity, but a supernatural one that comes from the cross of the Lord—that is, from the sacrifice that Christ offered on the cross. The cross, which was placed on Golgotha, is like the generator that produces electrical energy, which is conveyed immediately through wires and with lightning speed reaches very long distances to illuminate cities and villages. You turn on the switch, and immediately the electric lamp comes on. The same thing happens with divine grace. The cross, we said, is the generator of grace. The wires that distribute this invisible divine power, this grace, are the holy services, the holy sacraments, and most of all, the Divine Liturgy. Everyone's faith is the switch. If you don't push it with your finger, the light does not come on. Just as electricity comes from far away, so does divine grace. If you don't believe in Christ, the crucified Redeemer of the world, divine grace will not come to you. It runs through the mysteries, through the word of God, without interruption, day and night. If, then, you are not illuminated and do not feel divine grace upon you, you yourself are the reason, because you don't want to turn on the switch, to use your faith, that is, and come into communion with our Lord Jesus Christ, the fountain of grace.

We have said that electricity is invisible; so is divine grace. And just as the results of electricity are visible, so too all the results of divine grace. Those who believe in Christ feel the results. Others who are near those whom it illuminates, see them, too. The first person who experienced the results of divine grace was one of the two thieves crucified with Christ. One of them, the one on the left side, remained indifferent and unmoved, unbelieving and blasphemous until the end. But the other one, who was at Christ's right side, was moved by the passion of Christ; he believed in Him and said: "Remember me, Lord, when you come into Your kingdom," and divine grace performed its great miracle. The wolf became a lamb; the thief became a saint—a saint by the grace of the Lord, which takes the most sinful and criminal elements and transforms them into beneficial ones. Examples such as these are not uncommon. If you study the lives of the saints, the great *Synaxarion* (a book of the lives of the saints), you will find men and women who were mired in filth and corruption, and as soon as they believed in Christ, their thoughts, their words, their feelings, their actions, and all of their lives changed. They appeared to be new people. Adulterers became sensible; the stingy, charitable; the proud, humble; the blasphemers, worshipers of God; the unbelievers, believers. Whoever saw them as they were and whoever reads their lives today marvels and says: "This change was brought about by the right hand of the Most High." (Ps. 76:11 LX)

Yes! Divine grace is miraculous, and one of its greatest miracles is Paul. Because of this Paul says: "But by the grace of God I am what I am."

## NO ONE A TRAITOR

*Stand fast in the faith.*

—1 Cor. 16:13

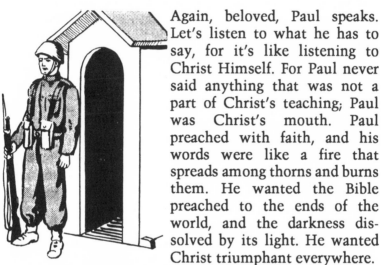

Again, beloved, Paul speaks. Let's listen to what he has to say, for it's like listening to Christ Himself. For Paul never said anything that was not a part of Christ's teaching; Paul was Christ's mouth. Paul preached with faith, and his words were like a fire that spreads among thorns and burns them. He wanted the Bible preached to the ends of the world, and the darkness dissolved by its light. He wanted Christ triumphant everywhere.

For this reason Paul was always at war; he fought every day. He called on the Christians to fight, too, under Christ's glorious banner. No one must leave the holy array. No one must be afraid. No one must throw down his arms and run away—or betray Christ.

"To the sacred struggle, everyone!" we hear St. Paul crying. Just as a brave general doesn't sleep while a battle is going on but goes everywhere encouraging his troops, this is what St. Paul does, for he is a general, too. But what a general! He is an incomparably greater one than any other general. He is a spiritual general. His sword is the word that he preaches—a sword that doesn't cut off people's heads but defeats and destroys every satanic thrust. And just as a general gives orders, Paul gives orders that Christians must carry out if they want to triumph.

We hear five of Paul's orders in today's Epistle reading. "Be watchful," is the first one. "Stand firm in your faith," is the second. "Be courageous," is the third. "Be strong," is the fourth. "Let all that you do be done in love," is the fifth order.

All of these orders were inspired by God. They are addressed to Christians of all ages and centuries. If everyone kept them, the Christian front would be invincible. We want our Christians to pay special attention to one of them because it is timely. It is: "Stand firm in your faith." With this order Paul admonishes us not to leave the faith, but to stand firm and unshakable, preferring death rather than denying our faith and becoming deserters and traitors.

"Stand firm in your faith." But what is this faith that we are called to keep until death? Let us give a few examples of it so that everyone can understand what it means. You get sick. You have a fever and pain. You are worried and call a doctor. The doctor examines you and tells you that to get well you must take medicine and go on a diet. So you take the medicine, you go on a diet, and you comply with everything the doctor tells you to do. That is to say, you believe you will get well because you trust the doctor. If, however, you have no faith in the doctor, then you won't take the medicines, go on the diet, or follow any of the directions. Faith in the doctor is the first thing a sick person must have. Thousands of sick people run to clinics and hospitals every day and entrust themselves into the hands of doctors. But are sick people the only ones who need faith? Nearly everyone's life is run by faith—that is to say, in the trust that one person gives to another. If this trust is shaken, a community cannot survive. Look around you and you'll be convinced. All who travel trust their lives to those who drive cars, trains, and airplanes. All those who deposit money in banks entrust their fortunes to strong, economic institutions.

People are always putting their faith in something. Those who have money, put it in banks; those who fly, in pilots; those who are sick, in doctors. And here is another example. Some people go to fortune tellers and put their faith in what they are told. But here is the tragic thing: While people put their faith in everyone and everything, they don't put their faith in God. God speaks to man. The words that Christ spoke and the Apostles preached and are written in Holy Writ are 100 percent true, and people should have complete trust in them. They should believe that Christ is the sole physician Who can heal them from that awful sickness called sin. They should believe that Christ is the only guide Who can lead them from earth to heaven. They should believe that whatever they give to Christ, even one penny, won't be lost but will multiply. No bank is that safe and gives as much interest as the bank that Christ has opened. It is called charity.

There were people in Paul's time who fought against the faith, and there are people even today who are fighting against it. As the end of the world approaches, unbelievers are increasing; they are fighting Christianity with greater fanaticism. They have a mania to uproot faith in Christ from the hearts of everyone, even from little children. "Believe in science," they say, "believe in mammon, believe in pleasures, believe in fortune tellers, put your faith in all of the devils, but don't put it Christ. Christ has nothing to offer you," they say. Unfortunately, many who listen to them lose their faith, leave Christ, and follow those liars, deceivers, and exploiters. They will meet a bad end: Eternal damnation awaits them. Not believing in Christ, the true God, is not only the greatest sin one can commit, but the greatest calamity. It would be a thousand times better for the sun to go out than for faith in Christ to be extinguished in the hearts of people. Therefore, for those of us who live in this age of unbelief and corruption, who want to stay near Christ and His holy Church, the Orthodox Church, which holds His teaching pure and unspoiled, let us pay close attention. Never forget that heavenly command that we heard today: "Stand firm in your faith."

## THE FOURTEENTH SUNDAY OF MATTHEW
2 Corinthians 1:21–2:4

# ENGAGEMENTS

*Who hath also sealed us, and given the earnest of
the Spirit in our hearts.*

—2 Cor. 1:22

This life, my beloved, has many sorrows, but it also has
its joys—worldly joys, of which one of the greatest is the
joy of a wedding. When our people say to a young man
and woman, "To your happiness," it is in reference to
their wedding. But before there can be a wedding, an
engagement takes place. That is, the young man and
woman who love each other and decide to get married
want to make this joyous decision known to their
relatives and friends. Their engagement is an official
pledge of marriage, and the engagement ring represents
an assurance that the pledge will be fulfilled.

The young woman who receives an engagement
ring is joyful and can't wait for her wedding day. There
are moving examples of women who waited five to ten
years for their fiances who were abroad. Mountains and
seas cannot extinguish love. An engagement between
honorable people is a guarantee of lasting love.

And now that we are talking about engagements,
let's talk about a bad custom that we write and preach
about frequently, even though many people don't want to
hear us. The young people, especially those in our
district, won't wait for the wedding to take place but
begin to live together as soon as they are engaged. It isn't
a rare phenomenon for the bride to be pregnant or to
have even given birth by the time the wedding takes
place. This practice is against the laws of the Church. It
is a sin. It is fornication, a shame, and an abomination.

It isn't right for crowns to be placed on the heads of a young man and woman who have lived in sin before the mystery of marriage has taken place. A church wedding means that the bride and groom come to church with virgin bodies and clean hearts. Christ blesses that couple who keeps the law of God, lives in harmony, produces blessed children, and sees grandchildren and great-grandchildren. May our young people understand what the Church expects of them, and may their parents, who, unfortunately, push them into sinful relationships, realize that no blessings will shine on houses where these kinds of sins take place!

A Christian engagement means that the young man and woman defeat the temptations of the flesh, contain themselves, and wait for the day of the wedding.

But why are we speaking about engagements? We are speaking about them, my beloved, because today's apostolic reading speaks about them. But what is this engagement that the Apostle Paul speaks about? It isn't the one that we know. It is a mystical engagement that is incomparably greater than every other engagement. When people hear that a poor, orphan girl has become engaged to a rich young man, everyone congratulates her. "What a fortunate girl," they say. "Now she'll leave her hovel and go to a palace and be its mistress and a lady. Who? The one who was barefoot and begged to live. That gypsy is going to marry the finest young man in town," envious tongues will say.

Yes, that gypsy is going to marry a prince! I am speaking parabolically. The young girl who is barefoot, hungry, and dirty is everyone's soul. And the son of the king, who is engaged to that poor girl, is Christ. Yes, Christ! He is, as our Church sings, the Bridegroom, the handsome Bridegroom. Or, as we say in the common language, the Groom. But what a Groom! A Groom who shines with beauty. A Groom full of riches, glory, and power. A heavenly Groom. Blessed is the soul that Christ shall love! That soul, we say, is engaged to Christ. Does it seem strange to you? Open up the books of the lives of the saints (the *Synaxarion*) and you will find girls like St. Thekla, St. Katherine, St. Barbara, and many others who loved Christ. They didn't marry but remained virgins until the end—not because they hated weddings but because they loved Christ above all and wanted to dedicate themselves to His service. That's why they said: "We are engaged; we have proposals of marriage." "To whom?" their relatives asked in astonishment. "We are engaged to Christ," they answered.

But someone might ask us: "Do you want our girls to remain unmarried?" No. We are not saying this. Girls who want to get married should get married. Let them start a home, have children, and live a Christian life with their husbands; they will go to paradise. But parents should not be afraid upon hearing that their daughters will dedicate themselves to Christ and live a virginal life until the end. The question is, in this age, is there one girl in a thousand who thinks and feels like St. Thekla?

When the Apostle Paul speaks about spiritual engagements, he doesn't only have girls who won't marry but dedicate themselves to Christ in mind. He has everyone in mind—every soul who believes in Christ. Is there a person who believes in Christ? Whether married or unmarried, poor or rich, white or black, red or yellow, or whatever color the person might be and no matter how great a sinner he might be, if that person believes with his whole heart and repents sincerely and gets baptized, his soul is connected to Christ and engaged to Him.

The engagement about which Paul speaks, then, is the close relationship that binds a person to Christ. It is faith. It is holy baptism. It is, generally, the grace that comes from all of the sacraments of the Church. A person who lives and breathes the atmosphere of faith and of the mysteries of God, feels a kinship with Christ and knows that Christ loves him and will not abandon him. Christ is faithful in His love. Whatever He promises He will give to that soul who loves Him, and that soul will be happy and full of joy.

But the spiritual joy and delight that the believer feels here in the world is tiny and small. It is but a fraction of that great joy that believers will enjoy in the next life. There, in that other world, blessed one, the wedding will take place—the wedding of Christ with those souls who loved Him and worshiped Him above all persons and things. This wedding will be unimaginable in grandeur. It will not be a wedding of the flesh but of the spirit. Christ will be united to the faithful of all times, and no one will ever be able to separate these souls from Him. And this union is called the wedding of Christ with His Church. Here on earth, the faithful only have the engagement. There, yes there, the wedding will take place.

My Christians! These are not lies; these are not dreams and stories, as unbelievers and atheists say. They are things that are sacred and sure. I ask you: Have you become engaged? Have you, that is to say, come to believe in Christ? If you have, then what Paul says today has validity for you, too: ". . . Who hath also sealed us, and given the earnest of the Spirit in our hearts."

# THE SUNDAY BEFORE THE ELEVATION OF THE HOLY CROSS
Galatians 6:11–18

## THE CROSS DEFEATS THE WORLD

*But God forbid that I should glory, save in the cross
of our Lord Jesus Christ.*

—Gal. 6:14

If, my beloved, there is anything for which a Christian should be happy, feel joy, and even be proud, it is the cross—the cross that the Church will call us to celebrate in a few days. When we say "cross," we don't simply mean the wood from which it was made. We mean the Crucified One, our Lord Jesus Christ, Who suffered the awful martyrdom of crucifixion. And with this sacrifice, He redeemed the human race from sin. Every drop of blood that was shed from the wounds of the Crucified One, from His pierced hands, feet, and side, every drop of Christ's blood became a river, no, a sea, an ocean in which millions of people are cleansed of their sins.

The cross! Without the blood of Christ, no one, but no one, no matter how good and holy he or she might seem, can be saved. Only those who believe in the Crucified Redeemer of the world are saved, cleansed, and redeemed. The power that comes out of Christ's sacrifice surpasses every other power. It is a mystical and invisible power. This power touched the soul of the thief and made him say, "Remember me, Lord, when you come into your kingdom." This power made the centurion kneel before the Crucified One and say, "Truly, this was the Son of God." (Matt. 27:54) This power also touched the soul of a fanatic enemy of the Crucified One and made him the most zealous preacher of the Gospel. He, of course, is the Apostle Paul. Filled now with gratitude, Paul falls and worships the cross of the Lord and says words that, together with the words of the thief and the centurion, constitute an eternal hymn to the Crucified One. Paul says: "But God forbid that I should glory, save in the cross of our Lord Jesus Christ, by Whom the world is crucified unto me, and I unto the world." That is to say: "Let others boast about whatever they want to; it's their right. I, however, boast of one and only one thing, of the cross of the Lord. His cross saved me. And He gave me the strength to defeat the evil that exists in the world. Evil can no longer defeat me. I am dead to the world and the world is dead to me."

What is this world about which Paul speaks? In Holy Writ the word *world* has a good and a bad meaning. The world with the good meaning is all that the good God created. It is the earth, the sea, the trees, the mountains, the sun, the moon, and the stars. It is the fish, the birds, and the animals. It is man, a divine creation. The world with a bad meaning is people—not all people, but those who don't believe in God, those who disobey His commandments, those who curse and blaspheme, and those who don't feel any remorse for the evil they do but instead try to lead others to unbelief and corruption. The leader who dominates this world with the bad meaning is Satan. This is why Satan is also called "the ruler of the world."

The world with the bad meaning constitutes a huge current of unbelief and corruption. It is a great and frightful enemy of the salvation of man. This world hates true Christians and tries to bring them to its side and make them its own—not to think, feel, or do what Christ wants them to do, but whatever this evil world wants them to do. This world uses two weapons against Christians: charms and terrors.

What are charms? They are the pleasant things this evil world has to offer. Money is one thing offered in abundance without work or sweat to those who succumb to the evils. Food and drink, drunkenness, loose living, and shameful carnal pleasures are other things. The positions and high places that this evil world is ready to offer to people provided that they fall down and worship it are more of the charms offered. And what are the terrors? They are the sarcasms, insults, deviltry, slanders, and threats against those who want to live Christian lives. The world is stirred up against them. In addition, there are the rejections, injustices, dismissals, persecutions, imprisonments, exiles, and in the end, a martyred, cruel death. These are the unpleasant things with which the world threatens. These are its terrors.

Alas, how much power the world has! Some people are defeated by its charms and caught in Satan's traps. They lose their morality and their faith and become part of this sinful world. Others are defeated by the terrors that the world uses against Christians. These people are afraid of the world and tremble before it. They want to go to church, they want to go to confession, and they want to receive Holy Communion. They want to perform their religious duties but cannot. They are afraid of what will happen. They have become so timid that they don't dare cross themselves for fear of being ridiculed by modern men. But glory be to God, glory be to the Crucified One! There are also Christians who are not defeated by the world. They are the crucified heroes of Christianity. They are dead to these charms and terrors, but they are truly alive. They have Christ in their hearts, and He gives them the strength to triumph over the world.

My beloved! St. Paul is distinguished among those heroes, those victors over the world. He defeated it, and no charm or terror could influence him. Because of this, and with good reason, Paul is heard to say: "But God forbid that I should glory, save in the cross of our Lord Jesus Christ." But us? Oh us who are defeated by evils and passions—we can't say these words. Let us then repent. Let us ask for the mercy of the Crucified One and make the decision to live according to His holy will until death.

**THE SUNDAY AFTER THE ELEVATION
OF THE HOLY CROSS**
Galatians 2:16–20

## CHRIST LIVES AND REIGNS

*I am crucified with Christ: nevertheless I live; yet
not I, but Christ liveth in me.*

—Gal. 2:20

We live, my beloved, at a time of frightening impiety, disbelief, and corruption. Would you like proof? At one time, if some stranger were to come to a village and blaspheme the holies, no house would open its doors to him. But now things have changed. Not only do the strangers who visit our villages blaspheme the holies freely, but it is nothing for those who live in them to swear and blaspheme them themselves. And blasphemy isn't the only sign of the terrible impiety of people to the most-high God; there are others who show that the world is not only impious but atheistic and irreligious. A young man, for example, who left his village and went to the university to study is very different when he returns. As a child he went to church, held a candle and the censor as an altar-boy, and helped the priest and the chantor. He was a charming boy who looked like an angel. But now he has changed completely. He has become an unbeliever. He has become a devil. In fact, he is worse than a devil because, in spite of his corruption and evil, the devil believes that there is a God. As it says in Scripture: "the demons believe and are afraid." But the young man who went to schools and universities and learned a few things about science and thinks he knows everything, now sits in the coffee shops and says to the villagers that science has proven that there is no God, that there is no Christ, that there is no paradise and hell, only matter. Of course, science doesn't say these things. Science, true science, believes. It believes in God. It believes in Christ. Great scientists who have worldwide reputations—astronomers, physicists, mathematicians, chemists, doctors, scientists of all fields—profess their faith and believe in Christ. But the young man whom we mention has never read what these great scientists believe. He thinks he's wiser than they who have spent their lives in science. He has the audacity to say that the Christian religion preaches lies and that He Who founded our religion, our Lord Jesus Christ, is a liar. There is nothing, he says. God died and we must bury Him.

That young man spreads the noxious influence of his unbelief to his fellow villagers. What do they do? Do they get angry and indignant just as they would if someone were to insult a member of their family? No. They listen to him without a protest. What does this mean? It means that faith in Christ is disappearing little by little, and that His name, which is above all of the names of angels and men, doesn't stir them at all. Soon we will accept whatever words come from the mouths of these wretched people who haven't learned the first thing about science. Seeing the coldness and indifference that most Christians show, unbelievers say and write that Christ died, and as the dead man that He is, He doesn't call for any response. Alas! A new belief is spreading—a belief in materialism. A faith in material things is now conquering the world. What a calamity! What a catastrophe, my beloved!

They say Christ died! But they are mistaken. In spite of the inroads that atheism and unbelief have made in our times, there are still people who believe in and love Christ and who are ready to shed their blood for His holy name. Who are these people? The little child who crosses her hands and says her prayers every night before going to sleep; the young man or woman who doesn't follow today's stream of unbelief and indifference but goes against it; the poor woman who goes to church and stands in front of the icons and, with tears in her eyes, says her prayers to God; the shepherd who tends his sheep and, hearing the church bell ringing, reverently crosses himself; the scientist who prays with a warm heart in order to solve the great problems of science; the astronauts who fly to the moon and bring Holy Scripture with them like an indispensable piece of equipment, which they read to take courage in their dangerous travels—all of these people contradict those unbelievers who say that Christ is dead.

No, unbelievers, Christ did not die. Christ lives and reigns. He lives and reigns inside His little flock, inside a small number of believing people. He lives and reigns in the hearts of people who believe in Him. He continues to have zealous followers in the twentieth century, no matter how few they are. And even if there are only ten of them, they are enough to prove that the love of Christ hasn't been extinguished, that His Bible isn't a book that has to be buried in libraries, as are other books, that His love applies even today.

The Apostle Paul, my beloved, more than all of the Christians of all times proves that Christ didn't die. Oh Paul! Christ was in his thoughts. He was in his feelings. He was in his writings. He was in his actions. Everywhere, was Christ. Paul was in continuous communication with Him. All sinful things had died inside him, and Christ lived in him. And he, who seemed the most unfortunate of people, was the most happy, because whoever has Christ in his heart has paradise. Whoever doesn't have Christ, has hell; it would have been better if he hadn't been born. Let us believe this, let us understand this: Christ is life, and death is the sin that separates people from Him. Paul, who lived in Christ, rightly said: "I no longer live with my evils and passions, but Christ lives in me."

# THEKLA EQUAL TO THE APOSTLES
2 Timothy 3:10–15

## A PROPHECY

*But evil men and seducers shall wax worse and worse,
deceiving, and being deceived.*

—2 Tim. 3:13

Paul, my beloved Christians, was the foremost Apostle. As we have said on another occasion, he was Christ's enemy before he believed in Him, and he persecuted Christians with fanaticism. Once Paul believed in Christ, however, he became Christ's most zealous and laborious disciple and Apostle. For about twenty years, he didn't stop working for Christ's glory. He went everywhere, to the east and west, preaching the Gospel. As a result, thousands of people believed in Christ and became His faithful and devoted followers.

In the end Paul was arrested and imprisoned. In the jails of Rome, waiting from day to day for the prison doors to open, not to be freed but to be taken to a place of execution, Paul didn't lose his courage. On the contrary, he passed the last days of his life with deep faith and hope in Christ. Of course, he wasn't idle in his jail cell. He wrote Epistles day and night. These Epistles were his last letters to his beloved disciples and to the Christians.

One of these Epistles is the second Epistle that Apostle Paul sent to his disciple Timothy. He had left Timothy at Ephesus, one of the largest cities in Asia Minor, to continue the work he himself had begun. Timothy had been ordained a bishop by Paul. As a bishop in a large, idolatrous city, Timothy faced many difficulties in fulfilling his mission. Paul tried to help him in the great task that he faced.

Among other things that Paul wrote to Timothy was a prophecy, because Paul was illuminated by the Holy Spirit and saw what was going to happen in the future. He thought it best that he make his vision known to Timothy, so that Timothy could be prepared for what was going to happen. Paul told Timothy that some terrible days would come to the world. Those who tried to live as Christ wants them to live would be persecuted and martyred. Evil and corrupt people, he said, would thrive.

They will thrive? Yes, they will, but what kind of progress will they make? There are two kinds of progress. *Good progress* is when someone goes from the worst behavior to the best. But there is also *bad progress*, or when someone goes from one bad thing to another that's even worse. For someone to make progress and become virtuous is difficult; many obstacles hinder a person from doing so. But in evil pursuits, a person progresses with great ease. The evil road is a down-hill road, and once something starts to go down hill, it is hard to stop. It is like taking a ball and throwing it from the top of a mountain that is close to the sea; the ball will start rolling until it falls into the water. It's the same with an evil person. He is like a ball in the hands of the devil, who can throw him wherever he wishes. The cursed one—the devil—will not rest until he sees the person falling into the deep and black waters of hell.

The people will progress continuously, the prophecy says, from bad to worse. The awful thing is that, while they are committing all these sins and crimes, they do not have a sense of their moral and spiritual misfortune; yet they think they are doing well. Sin will blind them, and they will not see where they are going. They are like the little donkey that is tied to the well-wheel with its eyes covered. As it runs around the well-wheel, the poor thing thinks that it is running straight ahead, even though it is really going around the same circle. In the same way, evil people are also blind and tied to the well-wheel of sin. They think that they are progressing, but they don't even take one step forward.

The people will progress in the wrong direction, Paul's prophecy says. Even worse, they will take others down the hill of error and corruption. Those who undertake to guide others down the road of life are blind in both eyes. Just as Christ said, "If a blind man leads a blind man, both will fall into the pit." That is, if one blind person leads another blind person, both of them will fall into a hole. But here is the stupidity of people: While they would never allow a blind man to be their guide, they willingly allow evil and corrupt people, liars and deceivers, and selfish and self-interested people to become their leaders. Those who are seduced by such people are as guilty and deserving of punishment for the trust they put in them as the liars and deceivers. Oh, how easy it is for the people of our times to be led into error and corruption!

People will go in the wrong direction, the prophecy says. Here are some examples. In a village there is a faithful, zealous priest who teaches the people and sets a good example. All of his parishioners should have confidence in him, listen to him, and follow him. But do they? No. A stranger comes to the village; no one knows where he came from. This stranger starts to say things contrary to those that the Church believes and the good priest teaches. The people should close their ears to what the stranger says and throw him out of their village. Unfortunately, some people listen to this heretic and become like him. Even worse, they convert another, and that one converts a third, and the third, a fourth. And seeing how easily they are carried away, one wonders how a stranger can convert people who had been taught the correct teaching from their youth and have before them shining examples of faith and virtue.

Here is another example. There are girls and women who respect the religion; they watch their behavior, dress modestly, and don't scandalize anyone either with words or with their actions. One day a woman comes to the village to spend the summer. Her behavior is indecent, and she is dressed—or, it is better to say, undressed—in seductive clothing. No woman in the village should pay attention to such a wanton woman, but all the young girls seek her out to copy her shameless ways. Such a woman can influence all of the women of the village.

Oh Apostle Paul! You prophesied that bad days will come, that evil will thrive, and that many will travel the down-hill road of unbelief and corruption. You, whom no power could induce to separate yourself from the love of Christ, intercede for us, we ask you, with your beloved Lord so that this evil may not influence us. The evil of which we speak is called evolution and progress by the world, but it should be called catastrophe and perdition. Yes, Lord, let us remain your faithful followers until the end, no matter what it costs us.

# SOWING

*He which soweth sparingly shall reap also
sparingly; and he which soweth bountifully shall
reap also bountifully.*

—2 Cor. 9:6

We are, my beloved, in autumn. It is the season for sowing. If you go to a farming village, you will see that everyone is in motion. Kelli is one of those kinds of villages in our district. It is one of the oldest villages in Macedonia. At one time in the past it was an episcopal seat. Now farmers and shepherds are its inhabitants. The village is in the mountains, untouched by modern cultivation; no tractors and threshing machines have made their appearance as yet. The fields are tilled in the same way they were tilled in ancient times, with wooden plows pulled by oxen.

Now, in the fall, with the first rains, the farmers get up very early and go to plow the fields. The farmer prodding the oxen is a beautiful sight. The plowshare goes deep into the soil, opening furrows as it moves along. When all of the field is plowed and ready for sowing, the farmer takes his bag full of seed and spreads it over all of the field. He doesn't leave any part of the field uncovered by seed. The farmer, faithful to God, crosses himself and asks His help before he starts sowing, because he believes that without God's help, no matter how much he works, his labor will be in vain. If the sky doesn't rain, if the sun doesn't shine, if a moist wind doesn't blow, how will the ears of wheat become a crop?

The picture of sowing in the village of Kelli, and in other villages that the tractor hasn't reached, is one of the most beautiful sights that agricultural life presents. We don't mean to imply that the modern way of cultivating fields—mechanical cultivation, as they say—is not good. Of course not. Machinery has made the work of our villagers much easier and more productive. But even so, a number of people are killed by farm machinery every year, and our farmers now water the soil with nearly as much blood as sweat because of the accidents. Farmers—martyrs! Oh you who live in the cities and sit at the table and eat the clean, white bread and other agricultural products, have you ever thought of the farmer who works so much? And beyond the farmer, do you ever think of God, Who gives them the strength to cultivate the soil and blesses the crops and fills the barns with wheat? Do you ever thank God that this small country is self-sufficient in wheat, while other large nations with vast lands have a shortage of bread and long lines outside the bakeries? Oh, people, glorify God and don't take any little piece of bread for granted. It is a sin and a crime to throw any bread away while millions of people go hungry.

But maybe some of you are wondering why I am talking about farmers, sowing, wheat, and self-sufficiency instead of explaining the apostolic reading. Well, I'm talking to you about these things because they are very close to you—you see them and feel them. And again I speak to you about these things because they are mentioned in today's apostolic reading. Did you realize that? Were you listening when the Epistle was being read?

Before I tell you what kind of sowing the Apostle speaks of in today's reading, I want to tell you one more strange thing. You won't believe it, and yet what I'm going to tell you happened. Listen. A farmer with a full sack of seed went out to his field to sow. But instead of taking handfuls from it, he took two or three seeds and sowed one far from the other. And again he took two or three seeds and planted them sparsely. He did the same thing over the whole field. Although thousands of seeds were needed, he planted only fifty or sixty. He didn't want to use all the seeds. He put the unplanted seeds in his barn. Guarding them there, he said to himself, "Can you imagine, throwing them all into the field! I haven't got seeds to waste. I don't care what others are doing, I'm not going to bury my seeds in the ground."

That's what this farmer did. But what kind of farmer would do something like that, you ask? We don't know anyone like him, you tell me. Farmers aren't stingy. They sow their seeds generously because they know that by planting one seed, it will multiply; one sack of seeds will become three, four, five, ten. Why, then, should they hoard seeds? That's why we tell you that these kinds of farmer don't exist. They would have to be crazy to be doing what you say.

And yet I insist that there are farmers who are stingy with their seed. Who are they? According to what today's Epistle reading says, they are the misers. Pay a little attention and you'll understand.

Money is like seed, and just like seed, it mustn't stay in barns but should be sown in the fields to multiply. Money must not remain hidden and useless but should circulate, and an important place for this to happen is in charity.

My money for charity? The miser will tell you he's earned it with much labor. Why should he give it to charity? I won't feed lazy people, he will say. But, Mr. Miser, it isn't a matter of the money being given to lazy people. Just look at the unfortunate people—poor widows and orphans, invalids, abandoned old men and women, unprotected girls, children in danger of taking the wrong road, women whose husbands have deserted them—there are so many cases of misfortune. Even philanthropic institutions need help—for example, the Red Cross. Give, then, to all of them.

But the miser refuses to give. If he is pressed enough, he might open his purse and give a little something—maybe $2 or $3—he who could give thousands and millions. The miser who doesn't give any money to charity is that stingy farmer we saw. On the other hand, the man who gives generously to charity and scatters money in the endless field of human misfortune and pain is the farmer who scatters seed generously in the field. The Apostle has these two types of people—the merciful and the miser—in mind when he says: "He who soweth sparingly shall also reap sparingly; and he which soweth bountifully shall also reap bountifully." (2 Cor. 9:6)

# PARADISE

*How that he was caught up into paradise, and
heard unspeakable words, which it is not lawful
for a man to utter.*

—2 Cor. 12: 4

Today, beloved, we will speak about paradise.

Paradise? Why did he select this topic, you are wondering. What century is he living in, you ask. Who does he think he's talking to, you say. We're not people from ancient times who don't know how to read; we live in the present—a time when science has made many great discoveries, when we've flown to the moon. He'd better bring himself up-to-date, and stop talking about hell and paradise, because people live better here on earth. He should forget these stories, you are thinking, because there is no such thing as hell or paradise; there is no other life. Paradise is here, hell is here, you say to yourself. People think like this and worse—who? Not just people who went to school and learned a few words—the rudiments of education, as Papadiamantes used to say—not just people who put on airs, strutting around like peacocks, thinking they know everything. Unfortunately, those unbelievers are not the only ones who reject everything. Unbelief has spread to all of the people. It has even reached the shepherds' huts. The most uneducated and ignorant people have been influenced by the preachings of these unbelievers and atheists, and many don't believe anything anymore. Most people are materialists! A priest who serves in a small village was telling me that an uneducated man, who was 80 years old, said to his wife: "You poor thing, what are all these things the priest keeps talking about? Do you really believe there's another life? Man is like the animals: He eats, drinks, sleeps, and dies."

What shall we say to all those who don't believe there is another life, a heaven and a hell? We have a lot to say. A lot of proof and arguments that great philosophers used to prove to the world that there is eternal life. Unfortunately, it isn't going to be possible to discuss the whole matter during this short sermon. Those who want to know what our religion teaches on the subject and why we believe there is another world should read the books that have been published on the subject. One book, *Beyond the Grave*, by Constantine Kallinikos, is particularly excellent. But we will only say a few words here, just enough to convince a person of good will. It isn't possible to convince the others who refuse to believe, no matter how many proofs and arguments they may hear.

We say, then, that there is another world. There is a hell. There is a paradise. How can we say this? Because someone whose words we have absolute trust in assures us of their existence. In no one else can we have as much trust as in the One who tells us that there is another life and that there is a hell and a paradise. Anyone can tell us lies and deceive us by telling us things that their imaginations create. Anyone can live in a world of fantasy, lies, and deception. Only one person out of the millions and billions of people who have passed through this world did not tell lies or deceive anyone by the smallest thing; whatever He said was true. He was not a simple man but the God-man. He is the One, our Lord Jesus Christ.

Our Lord Jesus Christ, then, assures us that there is a heaven and a hell. Where? Open the Gospels that contain the teachings of Jesus Christ and you will see. Especially study the amazing parable of the rich man and Lazarus in the Gospel according to St. Luke, chapter 16, verses 19-31. There were, the parable says, two people. One was poor and his name was Lazarus. The other was rich. The poor man believed in God; the rich man did not. The poor man had the virtue of patience. The rich man was pitiless and cared only for himself and how to live well. He was interested in nothing else. The two men died; the poor man died first, and then the rich man. Where did they go? Their bodies, certainly, were buried in the ground. In a little while there was nothing left of them but a handful of dust. But life doesn't end in the grave. At death, the soul is separated from the body and goes to another world. And the soul of Lazarus flew away and went to the bosom of Abraham. That is to say, Lazarus' soul went to a spiritual place to join the soul of the patriarch Abraham, a man who had always done good deeds and had died two thousand years before Christ was born. Abraham had died bodily, but his soul, being immortal, lived in a pleasant place. And Lazarus also went there. Unfortunately, the soul of the pitiless rich man went to another place, a place of frightful punishment. The rich man went to a place that burned with the frightening flames of hell—certainly not physical flames but spiritual ones, like the voice of the conscience of a criminal, which burns one's bowels like a fire. The rich man saw Lazarus in a very pleasant place and wanted to go there himself, but this was impossible. He asked Abraham to send Lazarus as a favor to cool him with just one drop of that immortal, spiritual water that runs plentifully in paradise. But even this was impossible.

This parable of the pitiless rich man and poor Lazarus, besides so many others, is great proof that another world exists, that there is a heaven and a hell. Because there are righteous people who suffer here in this world, and because there are unrighteous and evil ones who live well, it wouldn't be right that a righteous man not be rewarded or that an unrighteous one go unpunished. The justice of God demands this.

On another occasion Christ assures us that there is a paradise. When He was on the cross and one of the two thieves who were crucified with Him repented and asked Christ to take him with Him to His kingdom, Christ said: "Verily I say unto thee, today shalt thou be with me in paradise." (Luke 23:43) Christ was telling him, "Your body will die in a little while on the cross; but I assure you that your soul, which will leave from the body before the sun sets today, will be with me in heaven and will rejoice in paradise."

Yes. Lazarus went to the bosom of Abraham. The repentant thief went to paradise. But someone else went to paradise, too. He even went there before he died. He went and he saw things that the eyes of man have not seen and his tongue cannot describe. He lived there a few unforgettable moments, and again returned to the world. He himself testifies that there is a paradise. That person is the Apostle Paul. He himself tells us in the apostolic reading we heard today that "a power, a divine power, took me and carried me to the heavens, to the third heaven, to paradise."

Paradise is the dwelling place of angels, archangels, and saints! As a holy preacher used to say, "We can win you, but we can't understand you" (O Paradise).

# THE SUNDAY OF THE HOLY FATHERS
## OF THE SEVENTH ECUMENICAL SYNOD
Titus 3:8–15

## WORKS AND WORKS

*The saying is sure. I desire that you insist on these things, so that those who have come to believed in God may be careful to devote themselves to good works.*
—Titus 3:8 NRSV

The Apostle Paul, my beloved Christians, today exhorts all Christians to do good works— and not simply to do good works, but to be first in doing good works, urging others to do the same. But what, you will ask me, are good works? When the people in our time hear the word *works*, their thoughts go to the work engineers do, works that help cities and towns and the whole nation. They think of social, economic, and civilizing development. They think of bridges, roads, railroad lines, factories, tourist centers, beaches, hotels, schools, and hospitals. These kinds of works are done in all countries. Here in Greece, which was devastated by internal and external enemies who left almost nothing undestroyed, much of this kind of works is going on. The noise of machinery can be heard everywhere. Some might think that Greece has become an endless factory. Thousands of public works for villages, cities, and the state are being done. Millions and billions are spent on these works. In a few years, the experts say, Greece will be unrecognizable. Large factories, wide roads, apartment buildings, harbors, and airports will give her new life.

We are not contemptuous of the value of these works, because bridges, factories, and housing are needed. But all of these works are made of stone, iron, and cement. They are made with material things, and consequently, their value isn't as great as people think. They are works that can be destroyed in a few hours, even a few minutes. A strong earthquake can destroy a city that has the most beautiful buildings—buildings that took thousands of workers and millions of dollars to build. If an earthquake doesn't occur, there is the possibility that something worse could happen, something worse than thousands of earthquakes: a war. The fear is that it would not be a war with conventional weapons but one with a new weapon, a frightening weapon called the atomic bomb. A few of these bombs, say the experts, can make ruins out of the largest cities of the world.

We are not telling you this, beloved, to spread sadness and pessimism and to make people cross their hands in fear and say: "Since destruction is going to happen today or tomorrow, why should I work, why should I till the earth, plant trees, and build houses and factories?" Our purpose is not to spread pessimism and disillusion or to stop works of economic and political development. Rather, we want everyone to understand that the value of these works is minimal because they are, as we said earlier, material works. Sooner or later they will be destroyed, and nothing will remain of them.

More important than the works that many people marvel at are other works of very great value. These works don't impress people, but they offer priceless service to the world. These works have the seal of eternity upon them. They are divine works that elevate man and make him resemble God. They are works that the poorest and most insignificant people can do. They are works that are worthy of being called good works.

Good works! But does what we say seem general and abstract? Perhaps we should mention a few good works of the kind St. Paul talks about. Let us mention some from contemporary life.

A stranger comes to a village. It is winter. Snow is falling, and it is cold. If the stranger stays outside, he may die. If someone opens his door, welcomes him, and looks after him, this act of hospitality is a good work.

Good works! In another village a man becomes sick. He is old and lonely. He doesn't have any relatives or, if he has, they've left him and gone abroad and have forgotten him. As long as he was strong, he didn't need any help or care; but now that he's very sick, who is going to look after him? A compassionate old woman comes and looks after him for months. What this woman does is a heroic deed; it is a good work.

Good works! In another village, a poor man's barn burns down. He doesn't have the money to rebuild it or to buy hay for his animals, and winter is coming. But two good neighbors come to him and say: "Don't worry. We'll help you build your barn again. We will go to all of our relatives' houses and ask them to give you hay." And so, through their generosity, the barn is rebuilt and the man has hay for his animals. He glorifies God, Who sent those two men. Here then is another good work.

Good works! Do you want another example? In another village a man, the head of a family, is killed. He leaves a wife and children. His fields are untilled until a neighbor plows and sows the widow's field for no pay.

Helping weak creatures is a good work. This kind of good work, which hardly ever takes place in our times, was done often in the past. Villagers believed in God, and their hearts were full of goodness. Every Sunday after church, they would go to the farms of orphans and plow, sow, and harvest the fields.

My beloved! All of the works that we've mentioned seem small and unimportant in the eyes of the world, but they have great value in the eyes of God. The Lord will say to those who do them, when He comes to judge the living and the dead: "Come, ye blessed of the Father, inherit the kingdom prepared for you from the foundation of the world: for I was hungered, and ye gave me meat: I was thirsty, and ye gave me drink: I was a stranger, and ye took me in: naked, and ye clothed me: I was sick, and ye visited me: I was in prison, and ye came unto me." (Matt. 25:34-36)

This is the way the Lord rewards Christians who believe and do good works. Let us all, then, my dear Christians, do good works—the works of Christ.

# THE LOVE OF CHRIST

*. . . The life which I now live in the flesh I live by
the faith of the Son of God, Who loved me, and gave
Himself for me.*

—Gal. 2:20

In the verse that you heard, beloved, the Apostle Paul speaks
about a certain love, which if a
person doesn't feel in this
world, life isn't worth living.
But before we speak about this
love, we will speak about other
kinds of love that are in this
world. What is love? It is a feeling that's in the heart of everyone. Even he who seems evil
and debased has this feeling
inside him; he loves something,
either a person or a thing. Man
cannot live without love. He
will fall into despair and commit suicide. "Alas," he will
say, "no one loves me. I do not want to live."

Love holds the world together. It is the greatest
force in the world, even if it cannot be seen. Do you
know what it is like? Some night go out of your house.
Make the effort and climb some height and look at the
sky. What do you see? Thousands, millions, billions of
stars. The stars in the sky are numberless—that's what
the astronomers who search the sky with their telescopes
say. The more they study the universe, the more stars

they discover. There is no end to them. My God, what grandeur the sky has! Our amazement at the grandeur of God increases when we realize that the stars that we see are not as small as they seem but are very large. They are enormous globes, much larger than the earth we live on. Each one of them weighs millions and billions of tons. These globes don't fall but stay where God put them. They move within the space with unimaginable speed and make cycles that science calls orbits. These stars stay in and move in their orbits. Imagine millions and billions of trains running in the heavens, on aerial lines, and never running off the track or falling, but meeting their schedules regularly. The orbits that they make are so regular that astronomers know exactly when a star will appear and when it will disappear. My God, what grandeur the sky has. And in addition to the other questions that are raised by the sight of the sky, is this one: How do these huge and countless stars stay in place? Astronomers say that inside each of them is an invisible force. With this force one star pulls at the other, and the force becomes, let's say, an invisible chain that holds all of them together. This force is called gravity.

He was going to speak about love, you are thinking, so why are we speaking about stars and the gravity that connects them? It is because in the gravity of heavenly bodies we find a superb example of love. God hid gravity inside stars so that they can hold each other in place and move in an orderly and harmonious way, presenting the astonishing, wonderful phenomenon of the sky in the same way that He hid another gravity, love, inside the hearts of people to hold them together and create a harmonious and happy society. Although the stars obey their Creator and do not move out of their courses so that order and harmony prevail in the universe, not all people obey the universal law of love. That is why so much disorder, conflict, war, and misfortune exist in the world. As love diminishes in the world, happiness diminishes, too, and misfortune increases. The day that love disappears altogether because of evil and iniquity is the day that the end of the world will come.

Love is an unwritten law—a law put inside the hearts of all people—a universal law. Because of this, and in spite of the evil and iniquity that exist, there is still love in humanity. In this love, in this little bit of love that still exists, weary humanity finds some rest. Let's mention a few examples of love.

The nurse who stays awake at the bed of a sick person, offering care and comfort, has love. The mother who hasn't slept for days because her child is sick, who doesn't leave her sick child for a second, and who begs God with tears in her eyes to make her child well has love. The father who gladly consents to donate his kidney to save his dying child has love. The captain who stays in his sinking ship until all the passengers and sailors are safe but he himself drowns has love.

In mentioning one last example, let us turn our thoughts to the past. Fifty years have passed since the great Asia Minor catastrophe. The Turks had reached the outskirts of Smyrna. Hour after hour the barbarous enemy would enter the city to kill and burn. They were thirsty for blood, especially Greek blood and Christian blood. The Greek authorities and other leaders had fled. The Greek flag had ceased to wave. Only one person did not leave so that he could be saved. More than all the others, he had provoked the Turks with his fiery, patriotic preaching and had concentrated upon himself all the hatred of the enemy. He was Chrysostom, the bishop of Smyrna. Everyone begged him to flee; but he didn't go.

The good shepherd, he said, doesn't leave the sheep when he sees the wolf coming but stays with them and sacrifices himself. And Chrysostom was a good shepherd. He stayed with his flock and was martyred. He had love. Anyone who was there during those horrible days at the harbor of Smyrna and saw those hideous things remembers Chrysostom, the martyr of the nation, and is moved.

All those whom we've mentioned have love. But all the love, not only theirs, but all the love of all the people who have ever shown or will show love, from creation until the end of the world, and even all the love of the angels and archangels is small, very small, tiny, nothing compared to another love—a love that none of us feels as we should. That love, of course, is the love of Christ.

Oh His love! Paul felt it, and he understood this love. He would hear Christ's name, and all of his being would be electrified with divine love. Christ, he said, loved me and gave Himself for me. He sacrificed Himself for my sake. Christ, I love you. No one will ever separate me from your love.

My Christians! We love thousands of people and thousands of things. Why don't we love Christ? Why don't we love Him with a burning heart? That we do not is our greatest sin.

**THE TWENTY-SECOND SUNDAY
(THE FIFTH SUNDAY OF LUKE)**
Galatians 6:11–18

# A NEW CREATION

*For in Christ Jesus neither circumcision availeth any
thing, nor uncircumcision, but a new creation.*

—Gal. 6:15

Not long ago, beloved, a very
old man came to the Diocese
House. He was in his eighties.
He told me this story. "Before
I was even twenty years old,
your eminence, I was forced to
leave Macedonia and go to
America. There I worked very
hard. I did all kinds of work. I
created wealth and had a family. And, glory be to God, we
lived well. But then I got old
and realized that I was nearing
the hour when I would leave this world. I had one wish;
I wanted to come back to my country. And I came. I've
been here a few months. And how everything has
changed! The mountains and the rivers are the same, but
the villages, and especially our cities, have changed.
Before I left, the Turks were still here. Stink and filth
were everywhere. Most of the houses were small, like
huts. Now, new roads, new plazas, new buildings, new
schools, and new churches are everywhere. Everything is
new. Thessalonika, which was a stinking city in the past,
is now a beautiful large city. And our little Florina, how
beautiful she is! Our country has progressed a great deal.
In the sixty years that I've been gone, in spite of the
poverty, the wars, and the misfortunes that the land went

through, a miracle has happened. I thank and glorify God that a new Greece has appeared out of the fire and the ruins."

These were the impressions of an old immigrant, who came back after being away sixty years. From what he said, we take the opportunity to speak to you on the meaning of today's apostolic reading, which talks about a new creation for a new world.

Yes, it is true, out of the fire and ruins a new Greece has appeared in terms of buildings, roads, and plazas. This anyone can see, not so much in our small villages, which are being deserted, but in the cities, especially in Athens and Thessalonika. In these cities, whatever is old is torn down and replaced by new buildings. On virtually every street the noise of machinery that tears down or builds is heard. We have an unprecedented explosion of building. This explosion should make us remember Christ's words when He prophesied that the day would come when people will devote their hearts and minds completely to material things—to what they will eat and drink, how they will amuse themselves, what they will sell, what they will buy, what kind of houses and buildings they will build—- and doing all of this as though they were going to live forever in pleasure and leisure on earth. These wretches don't know what awaits them. These people are like the people who lived at the time of Lot in Sodom and Gomorrah. And what were Sodom and Gomorrah? Great, rich, and beautiful cities. The inhabitants of those cities had all of the material things they desired, but they didn't believe in God. Their bodies, their money, their houses, and their fields were their gods. They were slaves to the worst passions. Great thoughts did not come to their minds. Nor did virtuous feelings touch their hearts.

They lived like beasts—in fact, worse than beasts. They did things that animals would never do. Inside those beautiful houses the most unseemly and filthy acts went on. Only Lot's house remained untainted. These filthy, abominable people wanted to infect Lot's house, too, but God protected it.

These were the kind of people who lived in Lot's time. Did they go unpunished? No. The wrath of God came at a time when they least expected it. The heavens opened up, and fire and brimstone rained down on them, burning everything. Only Lot and his family, except for his wife, were saved. Whoever wants to read about the destruction of Sodom and Gomorrah, let them turn to the twentieth chapter of Genesis in the Bible.

What happened to Sodom and Gomorrah will happen again. It will happen, Christ's prophesy tells us, in a greater way during the end of the world. Large, beautiful cities will suddenly be destroyed; just as Sodom and Gomorrah were destroyed; because the people in those cities have stopped living like Christians. What are we saying? They have stopped living even like people; they are worse than animals.

What good are these beautiful buildings when Christians don't live in them? A cave with one holy person living in it is worth more than a large city with beautiful tall buildings that doesn't have people who believe in and love Christ.

Because of this, beloved, let me to ask you: Where do you live? I'm not asking where your bodies live. I know that only one dwelling place awaits us all, rich and poor: the grave. I'm asking, where do your souls live? Oh, if only we had divine eyes and could see where! Then we would see that they lived in a deplorable state that was full of filth. They live in a very old house that smells of mold and is full of spiders and reptiles. This house, which we never think of tearing down but continue to live in, with unclean spirits as our companions, is ourselves, our sinful selves—the old man, as the Apostle Paul calls it.

False ideas, superstitions, delusions, vices and evils, wicked thoughts, filthy words, shameful acts, thefts, prostitution, adulteries, murders, awful blasphemy, and other unclean acts—all of this is the material with which the devil builds our souls' houses. And with our consent.

Will your soul still live in this wretched old house, which is called the old man? Don't you feel sorry for it? You see to it that your bodies live in beautiful houses for the little while that they live, but don't you care about the dwelling place of your souls? Are you going to continue living in this wretched, old house?

Tear it down, a voice cries, and in its place build a new house for your soul. Let new ideas, new feelings, and new deeds, completely opposite from your former ones, be the building materials for this new house. Christ will give it to you when you truly believe in Him, sincerely repent, and ask for His help. You cannot build this new house by yourself, but Christ will build it for you if you give Him your heart. Then you will become a new person, "the new creation," about which today's apostolic reading speaks.

# RICH!

*But God, Who is rich in mercy, for His great love
wherewith He loved us.*

—Eph. 2:4

Rich? Who is rich, beloved God, and only God, is rich. God is rich? But what relationship, many will ask, has God with money? Don't be in such a hurry, and we will see in what sense of the word the Apostle says God is rich. The enemies of our religion, the unbelievers and atheists, in a book they've written to accuse our religion of supposedly supporting the rich and capitalism, were fooled by today's apostolic reading that says that God is rich. They said, even God is a capitalist! Oh, the blasphemy and the stupidity! Why didn't they pay attention? They didn't want to pay attention to the fact that God isn't simply called rich, but "rich in mercy." Do you know what *mercy* means? It means compassion, it means God's love toward man—sinful, wretched man. God, then, is rich in compassion, in love. Upon this meaning we will give today's homily. And, please, pay attention.

God is rich in mercy. God doesn't resemble the rich of this world, as the unbelievers and atheists want to present Him, and for this reason. The material things that the rich have are not theirs; they belong to somebody else. Whether fields, pastures, and plains, whether islands and lakes, whether gold and precious stones, whether buildings and palaces, whether factories and ships, and whether anything else that is at their disposal and they call their property, these are material things. Man did not create any of these material things. Everything comes from matter, which man takes, works, and makes into all of those things that are called technological progress. Everything is based on matter. And who made matter? Man? Why man cannot even make a handful of dirt!

The dirt we step on and despise is the most precious of all material things. Dirt contains mysteries. It has miraculous powers and qualities. From dirt comes grass, flowers, crops, trees—countless variety of things. All of the good things that we eat and enjoy come from the earth. Let the soil disappear, and then we shall see if the richest man in the world can live by eating gold and money! He will die from hunger. Man, consequently, has nothing of his own.

Everything belongs to God, Who created matter. But then, you will say to me, God is rich. Certainly He's rich, very rich. He is the only One worthy to be called rich. But how different He is from the rich of this world! God has no need of material things. He doesn't need bread, water, clothes, houses, ships, factories, or anything else. The ancient philosopher Socrates once said, "God is not in need." God, that is to say, needs nothing. He is a perfect and absolute spirit. And what He made, He didn't make for Himself. Oh, the love of God! He made it all for man. And He made it in abundance, so that nothing would be lacking. Are you hungry? Here is fruit from the trees; here is bread; here is milk, fish, and meat. Are you thirsty? Here is clear water. Are you cold? Here is cotton, linen, and sheep's wool. Are you sick? Here are herbs of the earth; here are medicines. Do you want amusement? Here is an endless theater: the beauty of nature, the earth and sky with all its grandeur. Do you want music? Here are the birds; here are the skylarks and the nightingales to sing for you.

To enjoy all of this, God gave you the means to be in communion with the world. He gave you eyes to see with; ears to hear with; a nose to enjoy the aroma of flowers; a mouth to savor the sweetness of foods; hands to caress what is beautiful and dear in this world. And did He just give man these means and organs only? He gave him others to climb to divine heights; these are incomparably greater than the five senses that distinguish man from all of the animals. Yes, God gave you a brain to think with, to judge with, to search out, to discover the mysteries of nature, to create science and civilization, and to become a small god. He gave you freedom so that you can choose good and avoid evil. He gave you a conscience to urge you toward the good and to dissuade you from doing evil, to praise you when you do good, and to censure you when you do wrong. He gave you written and unwritten laws: unwritten in your heart and written in Holy Scripture; written and unwritten laws to illuminate your way so that you will not get lost.

God gave all of these material and spiritual things to man. And man should have been grateful to Him for His generosity and love. Man should have made good use of all these things, spreading love and goodness to his fellow man. Oh, if only man would do that, the world would become full of good things and everyone would be rich, because wealth is the love that doesn't let anyone go hungry or be in need.

Unfortunately, man has not made good use of the material and spiritual gifts that God gave him. He used them only for himself, not to progress toward goodness, but to regress toward evil and corruption. Man wants to make all of those things that God destined for mankind his own; he wants everything for himself only. The center of the world for him is not God but man with his evils and passions! And thus man has become egotistical, cruel, inhumane, tyrannical, and criminal.

Man, who was created to do good things, fell from the heights into such an abyss that no one, neither man nor an angel or archangel, could save him. From where he was lying, no power could reach him. He was like a boat that had sunk in the deepest part of the ocean. But what do I see? Oh, the immeasurable love of God! I see an enormous crane reaching into that abyss and grasping him, raising him up, and plucking him out. From a slave to the devil, man became free, a beloved child of God. What is this crane that took him out of this abyss and raised him to the stars? It is the cross of the Lord. Written on it in golden letters is the love of God, an ocean of love, an endless and immeasurable love.

Do you see, unbelievers and atheists, why our God is called rich in mercy by the Apostle Paul?

# SAINT JOHN THE MERCIFUL
2 Corinthians 9:6–11

## SELF-SUFFICIENCY

*And God is able to make all grace abound toward you;*
*that ye, always having all sufficiency in all things, may*
*abound to every good work.*

—2 Cor. 9:8

Some people say that the Bible is only concerned about heaven—that we are people with material needs, and we cannot live according to the Bible. These people say the Bible is only for monks and not for us who live in the world. This is what they say. But what they say is not true. Christ isn't only concerned about the heavenly life; He is concerned about earthly life, too. He isn't only concerned about spiritual things; He is concerned about the material needs of people.

In addition to the other proof that we have about this, is today's Epistle reading. What does the Apostle say? If we are people of God—that is to say if we live the way God wants us to—we shall be self-sufficient. What does self-sufficiency mean? We shall have whatever we need to live, and something left over, so that we can do some good for others. Economy, charity—this is our program. And because what we say may seem like big bills, let us make them into small change so that everyone can understand it.

Self-sufficiency! The material things that a person needs to live are divided into two categories. Some of them, the most necessary and indispensable, are not the property of anyone; they are common to all people. These things are the sun, water, and the air. Everyone enjoys them. Can you imagine what would happen if someone could make the sun his property and sell its light to others? He would become the greatest owner of photoelectric energy. All of the power plants on earth today cannot produce the light and heat that the sun produces in only one minute! Millions, billions, uncountable kilowatts of solar energy bathe the earth. What do we pay for this energy, I ask you? Absolutely nothing. We don't even thank the Creator for it, as if He's obligated to illuminate us. And not only don't we say thank you: many people blaspheme God as soon as the sun comes up and they have to go to work.

The sun is a common possession of all people, as are water and air. But besides these common things that God gives in abundance, man has other useful and necessary things; they are food, clothing, shelter, medicine, and other necessities. These things, as we said in a previous homily, are made from the matter that the good God gave to us. But in order for man to have these things, he has to work. Man has to cultivate the earth, pasture animals, and learn various trades and sciences so that he can use this matter. God did not say that man was to be lazy and sit under a fig tree and say, "Fall fig, so I can eat you." God said that man has to work, and from the sweat of his brow eat his bread. Work is a commandment of God; it is the duty of people; it is a blessing and wealth. On the one hand, a small piece of land that is successfully cultivated can feed a whole family; an uncultivated valley, on the other hand, fills up with thorns and thistles and can't even feed one person.

In addition to labor, economy is necessary. Economy doesn't mean stinginess; it means a sensible and prudent use of material goods. Man isn't supposed to waste his possessions and spend what he earns in a week in one hour at a place of sinful amusement and corruption, because his family will go hungry. Economy doesn't mean wasteful expenses on luxuries. A person with little income can support a large family if he has prudence and economy. Another, who isn't prudent or economical but spends his money wastefully on unnecessary things, cannot support a family of only two people, even though he makes two, five, or ten times as much as the prudent person.

What happens in homes happens in nations. Some nations don't have many material goods, but they are self-sufficient and don't need to borrow. Other nations, with an abundance of resources, suffer because their people are wasteful. They are not self-sufficient. Would you like an example? Unfortunately, we do not have to look far; it's our country. In the past, Greece was self-sufficient in meat. Why? Because Greeks were economical and controlled themselves. On Wednesdays and Fridays, and certain other days, they fasted. They didn't eat meat. Now, most people have acquired bad habits. Money fell into their hands, and they threw it into good living. They cannot conceive of a meal without meat. They don't keep the fasts, not on Wednesdays or Fridays or even during Great Lent. And some don't even fast on Holy Friday. They've become like the crows that eat rotten meat. The result? The meat that the country does produce is no longer enough. Our country has to export currency in order to import meat from Bulgaria and Argentina. If only contemporary Greeks were economical, temperate, and kept the fasts, we would once again be self-sufficient in meat, as we are in other products, such as wheat and rice.

Work, economy, and temperance—these are the components of self-sufficiency! The Apostle doesn't want self-sufficiency so that money can be left over and we can become rich through greed. The Apostle wants self-sufficiency mainly so that any extra money can be allocated for charity—bread for the hungry, clothes for the naked, medicine for the sick, shelter for the homeless, financial resource for the treasury of the charitable organization of the Church, and every good work in this world. Self-sufficiency, then, takes on a greater meaning, a Christian meaning, and becomes a heroic creed in the life of the Christian, like the motto of ancient Greece: "Let us fast, so that we can give alms." Let us fast, that is, so that money will be available for doing charitable work. Unfortunately, in this age that we live in, this materialistic and carnal age in which waste, luxury, slavery to the stomach, and worship of the flesh prevails, there is another motto: "Let us live as well as we can, and let the others die!" Indeed, thousands die every day. If they're not dying in Greece, which has a degree of self-sufficiency, they die in India, China, Africa, and other lands. Where is our mutual support? Where is our love? Where is our Christianity?

My beloved! If we want to be Christians, let us make these four words our motto: work, economy, self-control, charity! In this way, the blessings of God will come to us. In this way, we will acquire a blessed self-sufficiency.

## THE TWENTY-FIFTH SUNDAY
## (THE EIGHTH SUNDAY OF LUKE)
Ephesians 4:1–7

# UNITY!

*Endeavoring to keep the unity of the Spirit in the bond of peace.*

—Eph. 4:3

The Apostle Paul, my beloved readers, advises us today to have unity. That is to say, all of us should live harmoniously like a family who has one father, God.

Unfortunately, the world is far from this unity! It is in a thousand pieces today. Where is love? Where is peace? Where is unity? In our century there have been two world wars. Nations were divided into two great, opposing powers. Cities were destroyed. Millions were killed and wounded. Millions were widowed and orphaned. Never have so much blood and so many tears been shed. Will that be the last of it? Nearly fifty years have passed since then. The United Nations, the world organization that was established so that nations would no longer solve their problems through wars but through peaceful dialogues, discussions, and the righteous judgment of all nations, is continuously shaken. Since the end of World War II, how many wars have broken out in different parts of the world? Several wars have threatened to spread their flames everywhere and start a third world war. Even now, as we speak, there are nations that hate each other. Their armies invade neighboring countries, killing and being killed. Always is the fear that their hatreds will lead to another world war.

Unfortunately, the United Nations, which promised to eliminate war and to bring peace to the world, doesn't have a sound foundation; it is an edifice that shakes. The League of Nations, established after World War I, was also shaky. It promised to solve the differences between nations and dispense justice, but it didn't succeed. Only the rights of the most powerful prevailed. When a small nation in Africa, Abyssinia, was attacked without provocation by Italy, and the Italians were killing women and children with their fighter planes, even dropping poisons to annihilate the people faster, this unfortunate country sent its king to the League of Nations to stop this evil. He went there to denounce the unjust attack of the Italians and to ask for protection from that international organization. When the king realized that nothing was going to happen, he raised his eyes, which were full of tears, and said the following words: "Lord of heaven and earth! The large nations have left your people unprotected so that a powerful nation may beat and crucify them. They expect help from nowhere. You remain their only protector."

What happened to that small African nation at the League of Nations is happening today to the small nations at the United Nations. Their complaints are not heard. Powerful countries do whatever they want to do. Small nations are wronged, and again the world is divided.

Not only have the small nations not succeeded in uniting and becoming a universal family, but inside every country the unity that God asks for does not exist. The people who live inside a country may speak the same language, use the same money, and share the same customs, but the worm of dissension is inside their community and continuously destroys it. In some nations in Europe and America especially, there is no fear of authority and the results are terrible. Every day we hear of strikes, riots, robberies, murders, and other crimes. The people hate each other. You would think they were sitting on top of a volcano that is ready to explode. The fire that is going to come out of it is enough to burn the whole world.

Perhaps there is unity today inside the family, but reality cries out that peaceful, harmonious, and unified families are a rare phenomenon. Among one hundred families, it is questionable whether you'll find one that lives up to the standards of the Bible. The rest of the families have no unity or peace. Everyone does whatever he or she pleases. Oh unity, divine gift, where are you? Where do you hide? We search for you in countries and in the large international organizations, but you are not there. You don't even exist inside communities or in families. Disorder, agitation, noise, disputes, and wars are the things that we see and hear. Women against men. Men against women. Children against parents. Parents against children.

Perhaps the unity that we are looking for is inside the Church; it should be there, at least. The clergy and laity who believe in the God-man should at least be unified, and no power on earth should be able to split them apart. All Christians should fulfill what Christ asked of the Father on Holy Thursday, when, after the Last Supper, He prayed: "Father, give unity to all those who believe in me, just as we are united in heaven."

In the first years the Church was united. As we see in the Acts of the Apostles, the Christians were like one soul in many bodies. Whatever one thought, they all thought; whatever one wished, they all wished; whatever one did, they all did. Never before had people had that kind of unity. The idolaters, seeing the unity of those first Christians, believed in Christ. Unity was a miracle that made a great impression on the ancient world and resulted in many people believing in Christ. Unfortunately, this unity didn't last long. A large part of Christianity broke it to establish papism. Again, papism didn't remain unified: a large part of it broke apart to form Protestantism. Even in our Church, the Church of Greece, we don't have unity; some of the people left because of the calendar and formed their own faction, that of the old calendarists. Not even the old calendarists stayed unified; they, too, broke off into different factions.

For people to be unified is a difficult thing. This is why, my beloved, today's apostolic reading counsels Christians to have unity among themselves. This is why our Church asks God at every Divine Liturgy to solve every dispute and discord between believers. Christians living in a divided world should be united; they should set an example of unity. Don't you hear what the Church is praying for? "For the peace of the whole world." Let us say it another way: Satan divides the world. Christ unifies it. Let us fervently ask the Lord to grant unity and harmony to our homes, to our villages, to our cities, to our country, to our neighboring countries, and to all of the world. Let our prayer always be: "For the peace of the whole world, for the stability of the Holy Churches of God, and for the unity of all, let us beseech the Lord."

# THE TWENTY-SIXTH SUNDAY
## (THE NINTH SUNDAY OF LUKE)
Ephesians 5:8–19

# CROSS-EXAMINATION

*And have no fellowship with the unfruitful works of darkness, but rather reprove them.*

—Eph. 5:11

Today, my beloved, a part of an Epistle that St. Paul sent to the Ephesians was the apostolic reading. What was Ephesus? It was one of the largest cities of Asia Minor. It was not far from the sea, and because of this, it became a commercial city. The Ephesians had lots of money, and wherever there is lots of money, there is corruption. Ephesus was full of taverns and sinful houses. The inhabitants of Ephesus lived sinful and wasteful lives, under the influence of wine, loose women, good times, fornication, and orgies. They were reinforced in their debauchery by their religion, which was idolatry. Their gods were themselves wasteful and corrupt, even worse than the people. They stole, became intoxicated, and seduced women. Since the gods were like that, you can imagine what the people were like. They lived in darkness, in prodigality, and in corruption. They lived like animals and worse than animals.

The true God, Who wants all people to believe and to be saved, sent the Apostle Paul to the idolaters. His divine words were a strong light—like the light of the sun that dissolves the darkness of night. The true light dawned in Ephesus. People who lived the most corrupt lives before Paul came, were moved when they heard him preaching. The eyes of their souls opened, and they saw the light, they saw the truth, they believed, and they repented. They shed bitter tears for the sins they had committed. They renounced idolatry, condemned Satan and his deceitful works, and were baptized Christians. Others, witnessing how the lives of these people had changed, were amazed at the power of this new religion and began to believe in Christ.

Some evil and debased people in Ephesus did not look upon this moral and religious change with favor. They hated the truth, and they hated Christ, because they didn't want idol worship, with its false gods, to vanish. Religion for these people was a kind of business. They made statues that they sold. They had taverns that would fill up, and they made good money. They had sinful houses that exploited women. But now, because of Paul's preaching, their shameful businesses were in danger of being destroyed. What would happen to these businesses if everyone became Christian? Who would buy their statues? Who would go to the taverns and the houses of sin and spend money? For these reasons, they hated Paul and would have killed him if the hand of God had not protected him from their anger.

Paul left Ephesus and went to other places. But even from far away, he didn't forget those Christians. He knew how corrupt that idol-worshiping city was, and he was afraid that the few people who believed in Christ would be overcome by the temptations and return to their old ways. Their relatives and friends would try to draw them back to their old religion with different and clever ways. It's like hearing them say to those Christians: "Oh, you poor things; are you listening to Paul? He's a fanatic; he judges things very harshly. It really isn't wrong to go to a tavern tonight and drink some wine and have a good time." This is what the devil always does. A small and supposedly innocent pleasure ends up being an awful sin. "Oh, you poor thing," they say to you, "a little glass of wine isn't going to make the world come to an end." If you give in, the one glass becomes two; the two, four; the four, eight; and in the end you will become a drunk who cannot be separated from his glass. Because of this, Paul advised the Christians not to become friendly with people who lived the wretched life of idolatry. He said that they should never justify evil acts but rather censure them with their words, and above all with their examples, so that any of those people who were well intentioned would repent and be saved. Reproval is like the bitter and unpleasant-tasting medicine that the sick person doesn't want to take, and yet this medicine is his salvation.

Without instruction, without the condemnation of evil and corruption, communities will rot and collapse. And woe to those communities that hate this censuring and persecute those brave souls who preach and write the truth.

In the excerpt that was read, Paul doesn't censure in a general and vague way, but condemns certain specific sins. He especially condemns one sin that was rampant in the city of Ephesus, and that was alcoholism. Every evening one could see people who were blind drunk, who didn't know what they were saying or doing, returning to their houses to abuse their wives and children. Paul shouts: "Christians of Ephesus! Do you believe in Christ? Were you baptized in His name? Do you hate Satan and his works? Stay away from the sin of drunkenness." A drunkard and an idolater are the same thing, but a Christian and a drunkard, no. A drunkard can't control himself. He does the most stupid, most disgraceful things, and commits the worst crimes. When he sobers up and learns what he said and did, he is ashamed of himself. And it isn't just that the alcoholic harms himself; he also harms his family. He leaves his wife in rags and his children hungry, spending his money instead to satisfy his addiction. Alcohol destroys health; it saturates the entire body with poison, and it eventually kills a person. The children of an alcoholic father are born handicapped, deaf, blind, lame, and mentally deficient, and tend toward depression and suicide. Unfortunately, instead of decreasing, the evil of alcoholism is increasing. In the past, even cities didn't have taverns; now the villages are full of them, and the people spend thousands and millions for alcohol.

Who is to blame for this situation, beloved? Many people and many things, but especially we, the clergy, who do not teach the people and do not condemn the evil. Because of our silence, it spreads. Who will control drunkards? Who will censure them and, if need be, punish them with spiritual penances? Who will make Christians temperate in all things with their teaching or by their example? Let that trumpet of the Bible, the lively preaching of Paul, be heard again in our land. Let his voice be heard from a thousand tongues in our cities and towns: "And be not drunk with wine, wherein is excess; but be filled with the Spirit." (Eph. 5:18)

## THE TWENTY-SEVENTH SUNDAY
## (THE TENTH SUNDAY OF LUKE)
Ephesians 6:10–17

# WAR!

*For we wrestle not against flesh and blood, but against principalities, against powers, against the rulers of the darkness of this world, against spiritual wickedness in high places.*

—Eph. 6:16

Don't lose courage, don't be afraid, but take your weapons and attack the enemy mercilessly! This is what the Apostle is heard to shout today. He calls us all to war. To war? "God preserve us," someone of the older generation said, just hearing the word *war*. He has endured the bitter experience of war. He was a child in school when he heard the sirens go off. He saw planes dropping bombs and people getting killed. The school closed; his teacher went into the army. His father went also. There was agony in his home: Will Father return? His family waited anxiously for the mailman to come to the village every day. When the letter came from his soldier father that high in the mountains the army was winning and continuously advancing, the child's joy was great.

The war ended. The child grew up, became a young man, and was ready to get married, have a family, and live like a decent human being. Suddenly the sirens sounded, again calling people to war. His father was now very old, and he himself was needed for farm work, but the young man could not stay. His country was calling him. With tears in his eyes, he left his old parents and went to the front. The war was harsh. Bullets were as thick as hail. The mountains shook. Men fell dead like wheat cut by the blade of a harvester.

At last the war ended, and the young soldier went home. He got married, had a family, and watched his children growing into adults. Now that the years have passed and his hair has started to turn white, he wants to enjoy a peaceful life after so much suffering and tribulation. But again the sirens wail, and he, who as a small child saw his father leaving for the army, who as a young man went into the army himself, hears the call for a third time. War! And he who knows from personal experience what a cruel thing it is, now sees his own son going to war, and his fatherly heart aches with the thought that he might never see him again.

The past generation! You lived in wars and heard "rumors of wars." It is natural for you to become uneasy when you hear about war. You hope that there will never again be another war and that there will be peace in the world. And yet, war!

The war that the trumpet of the Apostle is calling us to isn't like those wars that go on between nations. It is a different kind of war. As the Apostle says, in this war that God calls us to, we don't fight against the bodies of men, which are made of flesh and blood. It is a spiritual war, an invisible war; we have to fight against the most horrible enemies man has. Don't laugh, I beg you, when you now hear the name of those invisible enemies who fight against us. Only unbelievers and immoral and therefore foolish people think they can solve the questions of religion by erasing them with one stroke. How misguided they are! How deceived! There are more than just these things that we see in this world. There are unseen powers that have much evil and hatred for humanity inside them. If it were in their power, they would destroy everyone and everything, just so they could sit on the ruins of the world and laugh scornfully.

Laugh, then, unbelieving and wretched man! The time will come when you will cry inconsolably, and others will laugh at your calamity. Those who will laugh—let's name them—will be the demons—the demons who you say do not exist. They are your greatest enemies. For you to say that they don't exist is their greatest success. If you were in the army, you would know very well that the enemy is most dangerous when he can hide, when he camouflages himself. The army advances unsuspectingly, and suddenly, the enemy who has been invisible, comes out of hiding and attacks. The soldiers lose their courage; they panic and run. Didn't something like this happen to our army in 1912 in the hills of Amyntaio? The hidden enemy suddenly attacked, and a whole division was almost destroyed.

Satan's success is greatest when he's hidden. With his agents, with supposedly educated scholars, he spreads around the misinformation that he doesn't exist. And so people walk through life unsuspectingly, when suddenly he attacks. He finds them unprepared and destroys them spiritually. Had they believed that there is a devil who hates them with an indescribable hatred, who runs around like a hungry lion snatching souls, then people would take all of the precautionary measures that Holy Scripture advises them to take to defeat him.

The war against the devil isn't easy because Satan isn't alone. He has powerful allies who help him in his infernal plans; they are evil people, unbelievers who have never shed a tear of repentance, but mock everything. They are clever enemies who preach that there is no Satan, no hell, and in the end, no God.

Even stronger allies of Satan are our own faults and vices that burn in our hearts. Into this fire Satan throws his oil so that it will flare up even more. Satan goes from person to person and based on each person's weaknesses incites them to do this or that evil.

The power of the devil is fearful. But the Apostle Paul says that Christians don't have to despair, because they are soldiers of the glorious army of Christ. They have powerful weapons—spiritual weapons that if used effectively, will lead them to victory. Would you like to know what those weapons are? Listen as Paul names the weapons of his time. The soldier's belt is the truth. His boots are the eagerness and zeal for a Christian life. The shield that covers his body is faith. His helmet is what keeps his thoughts pure. His sharp sword, which makes Satan tremble and retreat,is his fiery preaching, which should be preached everywhere. If we were to add one more weapon from modern time, we would suggest the radio, which is prayer. These are the weapons of the Christian. Armed with these, the Christian can triumph in Christ Jesus, to Whom belongs glory and power. Amen.

# THE TWENTY-EIGHTH SUNDAY
## (THE ELEVENTH SUNDAY OF LUKE)
Colossians 1:12–18

# THE LOTTERY!

*Giving thanks unto the Father, which hath made us meet to be partakers of the inheritance of the saints in light.*
—Col. 1:12

All of us, beloved, know what a lottery is. Lately, many lottery tickets are circulating in our region. While many are sold by philanthropic organizations and societies, schools, and churches, the greatest number of them are produced and circulated in all of Greece by the state. The demand for lottery tickets is great, because all lotteries offer prizes as bait to attract people. If 100,000 tickets are sold, for example, 1000 of them will be prize winners. Some prizes aren't money, but different things like radios, television sets, sewing machines, refrigerators, cars, and vacation trips. The greater the value of the prizes, the greater the demand for tickets. Some prizes are worth millions, like the national lottery. These lottery tickets sell instantly. Is it a small thing to spend a small amount of money and win a prize worth millions? For a worker to earn a minimal wage, he has to work from morning to night; here, without any effort, he can win millions. His economic condition will change immediately. From a poor man he will become a millionaire. But where is that kind of luck, many ask. One poor man told me he had bought lottery tickets for ten years. "I spent so much money, but I won nothing. I will continue to buy tickets, however, in hopes that luck will favor me."

Why is the bishop talking about lotteries, you are wondering. Is he some kind of agent in our area who is advertising so that he can sell as many tickets as possible, you ask. We, Father, came to church to pray and to hear a sermon about Christ; and you talk about lotteries?

Believe me, I am not an agent of the lotteries. Our diocese has run some lotteries to raise money for a nursing home, a boarding house for students, and other charitable projects. But that is not why I am speaking about lotteries. I am speaking about them because the apostolic excerpt that was read today in all of the churches speaks about a lottery. I, too, would like to recommend to my beloved Christians that they buy a ticket, or better yet get one without even spending a penny. With this ticket, they can win not just money or gifts but something of priceless value.

What, then, is this lottery, and how can we get a ticket? If you are interested, beloved, be patient and listen to what we shall now say as we enter the main part of our sermon.

In Asia Minor, there was a beautiful city built near a tributary of a certain large river, the Maiandros. The city, called Colossus, had become one of the richest cities of Asia Minor. Its inhabitants, however, were idol worshipers. They were in the dark about the true religion. They were rich in material things but very poor in spiritual ones, because he who doesn't know and believe in Christ is poor and unfortunate—he doesn't know the value that faith, in the person of Christ, has for a man. But someone who believes will feel joy and happiness, even if he lacks all material things, even if he is hungry and thirsty, and even if the enemies of the faith throw him in jail for Christ's sake and want to kill him. The believer has an inner richness from God's grace, and he thanks Him Who made him worthy enough to suffer and become a martyr for the faith.

As we have said, the inhabitants of Colossus were poor and unfortunate, even if they lived in a large and rich city. They were this way because they didn't know the meaning of Christ. But then the blessed day came for that city, too. The day came when a poor man—the poorest of all but the happiest—came to that city. He came and preached Christ, and called the people to believe in Christ so that they could escape their poverty. The person who came and preached was Paul the Apostle. And did all of the inhabitants of Colossus believe in Paul's preaching? Unfortunately, no. We don't know how many people lived in that city. Certainly, there were over two hundred thousand people. Only a small portion of them believed—maybe one or two hundred, perhaps even three hundred. Those few who believed in Christ made up the first church.

Paul was moved because he found in this city noble souls who believed in Christ. When he was far from their city, he remembered them. His eyes filled with tears. I thank God, he said, for you who believe; for you who left that shameful religion of idolatry and all of those sinful pleasures and amusements. You who left the pseudo-philosophers, who never told you the truth but filled your heads with lies. You who believe in Christ are truly blessed. You have found a great fortune. You few have won a lottery ticket. It has been registered in the book that has the names of those who believe in Christ. You have become children of God, and as His children, you have become His heirs. You, too, will have a share of the kingdom of heaven, where the thief who was crucified with Him, who believed in Him, and who, before he died shouted with all his heart: "Remember me, Lord, when you enter your kingdom" (Luke 23:42) was the first to enter.

My beloved Christians! What we said about the lottery in today's sermon, we said to give you an interpretation of today's words of the Apostle, who, writing to the people of Colossus said: "Giving thanks to the Father, which hath made us meet to be partakers of the inheritance of the saints in light." More than nineteen centuries have passed since Paul said these words. The beautiful city of Colossus no longer exists. An earthquake destroyed it in the eighth century; only ruins remain. Where this beautiful city used to be is a Turkish village. Visitors go there and remember Paul and his heavenly words. Paul's words continue to have value and power for today's Christians, for Paul himself stands among us today invisibly, and calls us to believe in Christ, just as the ancient inhabitants of Colossus believed in Him. He advises us to get the lottery ticket—that is, to believe in Christ. Remember, whoever believes in Him and lives according to His teachings is the richest and happiest person in the world. We can say that this faithful Christian has won first prize in the lottery.

# THE TWENTY-NINTH SUNDAY
## (THE TWELFTH SUNDAY OF LUKE)
Colossians 3:4–11

## THE OLD MAN

*Seeing that ye have put off the old man with his deeds;*
*and have put on the new man.*

—Col. 3:9-10

In the apostolic excerpt that was read today in all
Orthodox churches, the Apostle Paul talks about two
men: one is the old, the other is the new. This is what he
calls them. Which of those two, if I might ask, do we
resemble? The old or the new? But before we answer this
question, we must give some kind of explanation to these
two words the Apostles uses.

*Old. New.* Don't think that these words have any
relationship to age. Someone who is very advanced in
age, an old man of 80 or 90, can be young. And again,
someone who is young, in the prime of life, can be old.
What, then, is this thing which makes one man old and
the other new?

In the common language, the "old man" means "no
good" (an evil man, a bad man in Greek). Calling someone that would make the person get angry, in fact,
infuriated and enraged with you. That will be the least of
it; it could get much worse. There are situations in
which someone hearing this might take a gun and kill
the person who said it. Everyone has a high opinion of
himself and won't let himself be called this. "Me, no
good?" he will say to you. "You better wash your mouth
out before you speak my name in that manner." Even the
most immoral person defends his name. No one wants to
be called worthless and no good, especially he who is the
head of a family and wants to leave his children and

grandchildren his good name. A good name weighs more than a ton of gold and diamonds. A good name is a priceless treasure.

The old man! And yet, my beloved, in spite of all the goodness that many people show outwardly and for which they are called good people, there lurks much evil and corruption. The old man is hidden in the heart of every person. A man—even one who is considered good—resembles a very deep well that seems clean on the surface until you begin to empty it and, upon reaching the bottom, see how much filth is hidden in it. A person is like this well. On the outside he seems good, but only God can see the corruption and evil that are hidden in his heart. Only those who have never taken the Bible into their hands and made it a mirror to see their evil and corruption—only they can say that they are clean and holy and that the name "old man" does not suit them, even though their faces are smudged. All those, however, who have read the Bible and know to what heights of virtue Christ wants man to reach and who realize how far they are from the ideal of the holy life that Christ preached and lived—only they "know themselves." Only they agree with Paul and are afflicted by the feeling of their own sinfulness. They kneel and call upon God to uproot the tree of evil with its many branches from inside their hearts and to plant the new tree of virtue and faith in its place.

The old man! Man, as we were given the opportunity to preach at other times, is not as he was when he came from the hands of the Creator. Man, as he was created by God, was a superb creation. He was like an angel. He was different from the angels only because he had a body. He didn't have any evil inside him. He looked at everything with innocence. He was healthy in all ways. And he could never die. This was man as he came from the hands of God. But alas! Because of his carelessness, the first germ entered into him. It was a germ that gave birth to the millions of germs that brought about so much catastrophe in the world. That first germ is the thing that scripture calls sin. Sin took man out of paradise and threw him into a bed of sickness. Sin brought pain and tears into the world. Sin pushed Cain into killing his brother. Sin armed and continues to arm people with knives and axes and other more terrible weapons so they can kill each other instead of living like loving children of God. Yes, sin changed man. Sin destroyed the angelic beauty man had and filled him with wrinkles and wounds. Sin made him unrecognizable, so that the angels, who see him in this deplorable state, say: "Is this the man who was made by God's hands?" St. Paul had this man of evil, misery, and corruption in mind when he called him the old man.

The old man! Do you know what the old man looks like? Imagine that a sculptor makes a statue from pure bronze. The statue is beautiful; it is perfect. When the unveiling takes place, everyone marvels at it. The sun's rays that fall on it make it glitter. But barbarians knock it down from its pedestal. It is abandoned, and later covered over with dirt and filth. It is buried for years, for centuries. But someone comes, digs, and finds it. It is in a deplorable condition; it certainly does not remind one of its original glory. But the sculptor who discovers it does not despair. He takes it and again throws it back into the fire. He melts it, and from its own material again makes a statue that is a thousand times more beautiful than the first one.

Do you understand what I'm trying to tell you with this example? I'm talking to you in parables. Man is that statue; a superb statue—a statue not without a soul but with one—a statue with a mind and a heart.

A statue is made by someone. But who made this statue that is called man? God made it. And whoever says that man came about by himself isn't in his right mind. A sculptor makes a statue. And man was made by the great sculptor who is called God. Statues are eaten by rust, and barbarians destroy them. And man? He is destroyed by the rust of sin and barbaric passions and is reduced to an unrecognizable state.

To this old man, then, this evil and corrupt man, this murderer and criminal, this fornicator and adulterer, who was full of evils and passions, came Christ, the God-artist. He took this man, threw him into the fiery furnace of His love, and from inside this old man, this killer and thief, came a new man, a saint. The world marveled and said: "Only Christ has the power to take old things and to make them new; to take coals and to make them diamonds; to take rust and to make it gold." To this Christ, the Creator of all, the wise Artist, honor and glory to the ages. Amen.

**THE SUNDAY BEFORE THE NATIVITY**
Hebrew 11:9–10, 32–40

# THE CITY OF GOD

*For he (Abraham) waited for the city which has*
*foundations, whose builder and maker is God.*
—Heb. 11:10

 Today's apostolic reading,
my beloved, speaks about
many people. They are people who belong to the Old
Testament. All of these people lived before Christ, at a
time of great unbelief and
corruption, and they awaited
His coming with great eager-
ness so that He could save the world. A great faith distinguished these people of the Old Testament. But of the
people that the Apostle mentions in the eleventh chapter
of the Epistle to the Hebrews, the person who excels
above all, Abraham.

Abraham was the leader of the Jewish nation; he
was the father, the patriarch, of all the tribes of Israel.
Abraham was the root of the large tree from which
blossomed the most beautiful flower, spreading its aroma
and invigorating the world. That flower was Christ. As
our Church sings during these holy days, He is the flower
"out of the root of Jesse." Jesse was one of the descen-
dants of the patriarch Abraham. It is worthwhile, then,
saying a few words about Abraham, that great man,
whom not only Christians and Hebrews honor, but also
the Mohammedans.

Abraham is worthy of wonder because of all his
virtues, but especially because of his faith. Abraham's

faith wasn't like ours: small, weak and lukewarm, likely at the first obstacle to bend and fall; Abraham's faith was a great faith, strong and unshakable, like a mountain.

Abraham didn't live in a land where people believed in God; he lived where the people were idol worshipers. His own father was an idolater. When the true God chose Abraham like a precious diamond out of the millions of people on earth, to make him the leader of a new people who would believe in the true God, Abraham didn't show any doubt or hesitation, even when God called him to leave his country and go to a new place. Abraham believed whole-heartedly in God's words and obeyed His command. He left his country, and for many years wandered here and there until he reached the place which God appointed. Even when he reached this place, the promised land, which was rich in material things, Abraham's heart was not influenced by them. He did not worship those things, like the rest of the world. He gave his heart to the true God. He believed in Him, loved Him, and worshiped Him. He loved God more than his wife and more than his dearest and only son, Isaac. Abraham loved God not only with words but also with actions and deeds. He was ready to sacrifice his son for God's love. He loved all persons and things that he saw on earth as the creatures and creations of God, but he worshiped none of them in place of God. All of these, he believed, no matter how useful they might be, were temporary. God is the only permanent, eternal, and immortal good. Abraham's heart was turned upward, toward heaven. Heaven is the eternal homeland, and Abraham wanted to go there in order to be with God always. Abraham had no greater wish than to be with God, to live near Him, to see Him, and to enjoy His love.

Abraham believed in God and therefore did not attach himself to material things. He did not build palaces and mansions or live in luxury. His house was a tent—a tent like the ones the Gypsies put up, which are here today and some place else tomorrow; no place is a gypsy's permanent home. This is how Abraham, the man of God, lived. He lived beneath tents, today's apostolic reading says, and awaited another world, the city of God, in the eternal life and kingdom.

Abraham lived in a tent. So what is the bishop trying to say, you wonder. Does he want us to live like the Gypsies in tents, you ask. No, of course not. I'm not telling you to live under a tent like Abraham. Our religion doesn't prohibit you from building a house for your family and living in some comfort; what it prohibits is giving your whole heart to material things, and thinking that joy and happiness come from them.

You can live in a tent, and in spite of it, if there is love between you and your spouse and children, you can be the happiest person in the world. You can live in a palace like a lord and king, and yet, if you don't have love between you and your family, you can be very miserable. A person is a heart, not land, buildings, cars, factories, and machinery. Have you given your heart to God? Then you are happy. If you haven't given it to Him, did you give it to people and things of the world? Even if you think that you are happy, a day will come when you will be sad. For something will come and take it all away from you. That something is death. Is there anything that's permanent and unchanged in the world, beloved?

Look at the city or village that you live in. Don't look only at the huts of the poor, but at the mansions of the rich, which were built with so much effort. I ask you: Who were the people living in these large houses one hundred years ago? Alas! They who built them are no longer there. They live somewhere else now; they live in the cemetery. They live in a small house whose length is 2 meters and whose width is 1 meter; they live in a grave. Their bodies—certainly not their souls—will become dust in a little while. How right was a monk when he wrote in large letters on the front of his cell, "My cell, my cell, today you are mine, tomorrow of another, and never anyone's," so that he could read it every day and remember the vanity of the world.

Astronauts in their spaceships can see the earth as something that is very small, like a ball that children play with. The higher they fly, the smaller it will seem. The earth, with all its large cities and countries, and all its goods, is like a grain of sand. And for this, then, this grain of sand, which will also disappear one day, there is so much evil, so much hatred, so much malice, so many wars, so much blood, and so many tears. Certainly, the world which is far away from God looks like it has gone crazy and worshiped creation, not the Creator, the Creator of all.

My beloved Christians! How long will we have our eyes fixed on this vain and sinful world? Abraham calls us today, thousands of saints call us today, and the Church calls us today: "Let us lift up our hearts." For we, too, can reach heaven and go higher than the astronauts, to an immaterial and spiritual world.

Christ opened the road, the avenue to heaven. This road is called the road of repentance. Believe, repent, and be saved, brothers and sisters.

## THE SUNDAY BEFORE EPIPHANY
2 Timothy 4:5–8

## WHERE ARE OUR SACRIFICES?

*For I am already being poured out as a drink offering,
and the time of my departure is at hand.*
—2 Tim. 4:6

Today, my beloved, is the Sunday before Epiphany. And today we will examine the last apostolic excerpt in this book. We will take one word out of it, and attempt to interpret it, for one word out of the Bible is enough to teach us the greatest lessons and bring us closer to God. What is written in Holy Scripture is inspired by God. The Bible can teach man, if he's not biased against it and thinks that it's just another book whose writers can err. Happy is he who hears it, reads it with faith, and tries to practice what it says. Whoever doesn't believe in it and lives contrary to what it teaches is like Judas, who betrayed Christ. It would have been better for Judas had he never been born. Whoever listens to the word of God and believes in it is a true human being.

Let's listen, then, to the Apostle Paul. From his blessed mouth comes a word—a word that is like a pearl, a diamond, even. That word is *Spendomai* in Greek. It means "I am being poured out."

*Spendomai.* To understand what St. Paul meant when he used this word, we first have to tell you what this expression meant in ancient times. In those days, people lived in the darkness of idolatry. Their gods, those lifeless idols, were false. However, the ancients believed in them and honored and worshiped them. As a way of honoring them, they offered sacrifices.

We worship God today; we go to church and express our worship by lighting candles, burning incense, and offering olive oil and bread. But the idol worshipers offered another kind of sacrifice. They would gather at the altar and offer sheep, goats, and oxen. They would light fires on their altars, and their priests would slaughter the animals and burn them. At this point, the priest would fill a golden goblet with wine or with blood from the animal that had been sacrificed, and pour it on the altar. This practice was called a *sponde* in Greek, or a libation.

A *sponde* often took place when two cities or nations made an alliance and promised to help each other in times of trouble. To seal the alliance, the representatives of the cities or nations would offer a sacrifice and make libations. If one of them did not keep the treaty, that party was said to *parespondese;* in ancient times, this word was worse than the word "betray," for the one who had violated the treaty had deceived the gods; such people were not only considered traitors but also impious.

Paul takes this passion from the ancient world and gives it a new, superb meaning. "I am being poured out," he writes to his beloved disciple Timothy.

If we analyze this word "spendomai" in terms of the way Paul uses it, it means the following: Life is like a cup that the good God fills up. To one He gives more, to another less. But no one goes without some blessings in proportion to his or her spiritual strength, in proportion to what his or her cup will hold. God fills all of these cups. Health, intelligence, ability, scholarship, esteem, friendships and relationships, marriage, a family, material and spiritual goods—such are what the cup of life contains. God gives us these blessings to use for our own good, for the good of our neighbor, and for His glory. But how do people use these material and spiritual blessings?

Do they use them for their own good? For the good of humanity? For the glory of God?

Today is the last Sunday of the year, and everyone should be in church thanking God Who gave them another year of life. But today the church has very few Christians in it. Most people are out on the streets or in the squares. They are selling and buying so that they can celebrate New Year's Day. They don't give a thought to God. Nor is this all of it. When the day is over, people will gather in their houses and play cards all night. Purses and wallets full of money will empty. Exorbitant amounts of money will be lost. In the morning hours, while the church bells are ringing, they will be returning to their homes penniless, full of disgust and exasperation. They have been up all night; they have wasted precious time; they have damaged their health; they have hated their fellow man; they have blasphemed; they have lost much money. To whom, I ask you, did they offer this money as a sacrifice? They wouldn't have given some unfortunate family a small financial donation. What am I saying? They wouldn't have given them anything. And they wouldn't have given any to Christ either; remember, Christ is hidden behind every unfortunate person. They wouldn't sacrifice a penny to Him; but to the cards—to the goddess of chance, as they say—and because there is no such thing as chance but the devil—to the devil, then, who carries a pack of cards with him, to him they make the libation, the *sponde*, with their money on New Year's Day. To the devil they sacrifice millions. We could mention many other examples from contemporary life to show where people make their libations (*spondas*). To say that today's people offer up virtually all of their material and spiritual goods as a sacrifice to the devil is no exaggeration.

But glory be to God! There are souls who sacrifice whatever God has given to them for His glory. They keep nothing for themselves. They give everything that they have to their fellow men who are in need. They give everything to God!

Paul the Apostle comes first in this catalogue of heroes. He was a young man who was descended from nobility. He was educated and knew many languages. He had Roman citizenship. He was active and clever and could have succeeded anywhere, in any art and science, and become rich and famous. The cup of his life was filled with priceless gifts. But he sacrificed them all. For thirty years he traveled throughout his region, preaching Christ without receiving any compensation whatsoever, but rather living from his everyday labors in a constant state of danger, even. Finally, he was imprisoned in the jails of Rome, awaiting his death. The cup of his life had almost emptied. A few drops of it remained. But he wasn't anxious or afraid. Instead, he eagerly awaited that blessed hour when he would be sacrificed, when he would shed even his last drop of blood for Christ, Whom he loved above everyone and everything. And during this holy waiting period, he could not find a better word to express the feelings in his heart than the word "spendomai": "I am being poured out, Christ, I've sacrificed everything for You; now I even sacrifice my life."

Oh Paul, blessed Paul! You sacrificed everything for Christ. But what about us? Where are our sacrifices? Let us weep, because this heroic element is missing in us. And let us make this our resolution for the New Year: We will give nothing to the devil; we will give everything to Christ.

# INDEX